NAMING WHAT WE KNOW

NAMING WHAT WE KNOW

Threshold Concepts of Writing Studies
CLASSROOM EDITION

Edited by
LINDA ADLER-KASSNER
ELIZABETH WARDLE

UTAH STATE UNIVERSITY PRESS
Logan

© 2016 by the University Press of Colorado

Published by Utah State University Press
An imprint of University Press of Colorado
5589 Arapahoe Avenue, Suite 206C
Boulder, Colorado 80303

 The University Press of Colorado is a proud member of
The Association of American University Presses.

The University Press of Colorado is a cooperative publishing enterprise supported, in part, by Adams State University, Colorado State University, Fort Lewis College, Metropolitan State University of Denver, Regis University, University of Colorado, University of Northern Colorado, Utah State University, and Western State Colorado University.

∞ The paper used in this publication meets the minimum requirements of the American National Standard for Information Sciences – Permanence of Paper for Printed Library Materials. ANSI Z39.48-1992

ISBN: 978-1-60732-577-2 (paper)
ISBN: 978-1-60732-578-9 (ebook)

Library of Congress Cataloging-in-Publication Data

Names: Adler-Kassner, Linda, editor. | Wardle, Elizabeth A., editor.
Title: Naming what we know : threshold concepts of writing studies / edited by Linda Adler-Kassner, Elizabeth Wardle.
Description: Classroom edition. | Logan : Utah State University Press, [2015] | Includes bibliographical references.
Identifiers: LCCN 2016014716 | ISBN 9781607325772 (pbk.) | ISBN 9781607325789 (ebook)
Subjects: LCSH: English language—Composition and exercises—Study and teaching (Higher)—United States. | English language—Rhetoric—Study and teaching (Higher)—United States.
Classification: LCC PE1405.U6 N36 2015 | DDC 808/.042071—dc23
LC record available at https://lccn.loc.gov/2016014716

CONTENTS

PREFACE

As learners (and teachers and researchers), both of us have had learning experiences that have transformed us. For Linda, one experience came in an introductory communication theory seminar, when she realized that standards of time and measurement were culture- and value-laden. Ultimately, this led to the realization that other standards—like those used to place student writers—were just as connected to culture and values . . . but sometimes not the student writer's own. For Elizabeth, one experience came when she was introduced to the idea of theory, and particularly feminist theory, in her first-year writing class, and then again in upper-level courses—theory that helped her see her own experiences and positionality in an entirely new way. Looking back on those learning experiences, we now can recognize them as encounters with "threshold concepts."

Originally identified by researchers J. F. Meyer and Ray Land (2006), threshold concepts are ideas that learners must "see through and see with" (Kreber 2009, 11) in order to participate more fully in particular disciplines. Meyer and Land have identified characteristics that are associated with learners' encounters with threshold concepts, noting that they are:

- *Troublesome.* These concepts may be conceptually difficult and butt up against prior knowledge that is inert, contradictory, rarely used, or unchallenged. They may also ask learners to take on new identities that are uncomfortable.
- *Liminal.* Threshold concepts involve what the name implies—thresholds. But the movement toward and the (hopeful) crossing of those thresholds isn't straightforward; instead, it happens in a two-steps-forward-one-step-back kind of way as learners push against troublesome knowledge.
- *Integrative and transformative.* Once learners cross a threshold, their ability to see through and with a threshold concept leads them to recognize new patterns of meaning around that concept. The ability to see through and with that concept also transforms their understandings of phenomena, people, and/or events.

- *Probably irreversible.* Once a learner begins to see through and with a threshold concept, it's very difficult to "unlearn" or "unsee" through that lens.

It is important to note that threshold concepts are not core concepts. Core concepts might be understood as building blocks for understanding—necessary but not transformative. Threshold concepts, on the other hand, are more than "core" or foundational. They are ideas, ways of seeing, ways of understanding that change a learner's stance. They help that learner see things differently and make connections across sites and ideas that previously might have seemed unconnected. In other words, learning threshold concepts doesn't just change *what* people know; they change how people know because they lead to different ways of approaching ideas by thinking through and with these concepts.

In considering the difference between core concepts and threshold concepts, it might help to look at an example. "Discourse community" might be understand as a core concept or an important key term for writing studies. Learning this term might be an important building block, but being able to define discourse community does not in and of itself change anything in the learner's stance, view, or behavior. On the other hand, a related and underlying threshold concept might be that knowledge is socially constructed and that groups of people use language together in particular ways that reflect what they know and do, and that language use in turn impacts who they are and how they behave. This collection, in fact, features a number of threshold concepts related to this way of understanding the relationships between individuals, language, and practices. Really grasping these ideas takes a long time, but if learners do come to understand them, they are likely to change how they see and understand what people are doing together, how they are using language to do it, and what they might do when joining new workplaces, classrooms, or other groups. Clearly, though, learning this threshold concept is much more complex than learning a key term or core concept. It takes time, struggle, and experience. Learning a threshold concept, in fact, might entail *unlearning* previous ideas about how language works and what groups of people do together with language. Meyer and Land emphasize the ways that threshold concepts are troublesome because they are conceptually difficult or conflict with prior knowledge or "common sense" views of a subject—or they ask learners to be and do something that they may not be comfortable with. Thus, the time it takes to learn threshold concepts can be quite extended—and unsettling for both learners and teachers.

We certainly recognize these features when we look back on our own encounters with threshold concepts. As we've conducted research on others' experiences with these concepts—both faculty and students— we see these characteristics reflected in their experiences, as well. The *idea* of threshold concepts thus seems to identify what is happening as learners move through different sites of learning. As teachers of writing working with students in our individual writing classes, then, threshold concepts seems to be a productive frame for thinking about students' experiences.

At the same time, we've also introduced threshold concepts to undergraduate and graduate students with whom we've worked. (In fact, one root of this collection lies in graduate "Theory and Practice of Academic Writing" courses taken by graduate students learning to teach first year writing.) Just as we have found threshold concepts to be a useful way for us to consider student experiences, we've found that our students (graduate and undergraduate) have found threshold concepts useful in two ways. First, they've found the *idea* of threshold concepts productive, as it provides a structure through which to understand how learning is organized within higher education. That is: faculty tend to structure their ideas of learning through threshold concepts, and these concepts are woven throughout courses—from lectures to assignments. When students recognize that threshold concepts are part of what form the infrastructure of their learning, it helps them to find ways to make that infrastructure more visible and explicit, when it is typically fairly invisible or tacit, (see Bowker and Star [1999] on the idea of invisibility and infrastructures). Second, they've found that the threshold concepts of writing studies provide a lens through which they can begin to grapple with writing studies/composition courses, especially those focusing on writing as an activity and a subject of study (see threshold concept 1 in this collection). Graduate students, especially, have also found that these threshold concepts provide a way to think about writing within and across disciplines. For all of these reasons, then, we think that the struggle (or troublesomeness) involved with the sometimes messy learning of threshold concepts is not just well worth the effort, but it is critical for learners and teachers.

Before you begin to work with the threshold concepts in this collection, we want to point out that threshold concepts about writing are a little different than threshold concepts of some other disciplines. Whereas students in a physics class may be learning threshold concepts that do not necessarily apply if they leave the study of physics, the same cannot be said about the threshold concepts of writing. Everybody writes, and so much of what we know as a field about writing is relevant and help-ful to all writers, whether they are just passing through a writing class or preparing to finish a Ph.D. in writing studies. In addition, because writ-ing is a means of learning, it is often included in conversations about student learning generally, well beyond writing classrooms. Discussions about students' abilities in public media seem to always include "writ-ing" or "communication." Policy documents attempting to outline what students should learn, how that learning should be fostered or shaped, and how learning should be assessed almost always attend to writing (e.g., the new SAT; the Common Core Standards; AAC&U's LEAP; the Degree Qualifications Profile).

Many in our field have decried the ways that writing and writers are portrayed in broader media and policy discussions of writing, complain-ing that they do not reflect the research-based knowledge of our disci-pline. Sometimes, as a field, we have not always been very successful at explaining to stakeholders what we know and bring to the table. But the two of us have witnessed (and participated in) work that that has attempted to articulate our field's knowledge and consider its relation-ship to practice in a variety of contexts, from teaching to policy, within the field. Part of our motivation for the project of *Naming What We Know: Threshold Concepts in Writing Studies* was to try to provide a method and site where writing scholars could do more of the latter, and perhaps find new and innovative ways of impacting media and policy discussions of writing, as well as the everyday practices that influence writers—espe-cially students. In other words, we hoped that by asking colleagues to simply and clearly articulate some of what we know about writing, we might find ways to better explain that knowledge to stakeholders and students, in ways that might have positive impacts.

The idea of the project was relatively simple: We invited forty-five colleagues from the field to attempt to collectively define threshold concepts of our discipline. To help them do this, we distributed the introduction to Meyer and Land's first book, *Overcoming Barriers to Student Understanding*, and set up a wiki. Eventually, twenty-nine of the original forty-five participants stayed with the project. Our collaborators (and we) then tried to name some threshold concepts from our disci-pline, made fifty-one suggestions regarding what they considered to be threshold concepts, and wrote 139 comments regarding the concepts proposed by others. The two of us then met and analyzed the wiki con-tributions. We distilled one meta-concept, *writing is a subject of study and an activity*, and five overarching concepts that seemed to unfold into somewhere between three and nine constituent elements. We circulated this draft with the participants; after their revisions and approval, we assigned contributors to write extended definitions (1000-word definitions for overarching concepts and 500-word definitions for the sub-concepts). Some of these authors took on co-authors at this stage who had not participated in previous stages but who were experts in the concept at hand. Resulting drafts were revised and posted to the wiki. Several concepts were revised, moved, integrated with others, or deleted altogether before the current concepts and categories were finalized.

In the end, we collectively agreed upon thirty-six threshold concepts and produced a book, *Naming What We Know*, that included these concepts along with eight essays that considered in more depth the ways in which these concepts contributed to thinking and work in key points in the field. We're pleased that Utah State University Press and University Press of Colorado have chosen also to produce this shorter version of our book, which includes only the threshold concepts. The purpose of this shorter version is to make the book more approachable for classroom use, giving students and other newcomers to the field a quick entry point to some of the often unstated beliefs about writing that our field has come to agree on after decades of research and theory.

Of course, reading about a threshold concept is in no way equivalent to *learning* the threshold concept. Learners who are new to the field might have varied reactions to the threshold concepts that are summarized here. One reaction might be: "This is so obvious." At first glance, many summarized threshold concepts seem "obvious." It is only upon actually attempting to enact the ideas of those concepts that learners recognize how truly difficult they are. For example, one of the threshold concepts in this book is that failure is an important part of learning to write. Many readers might respond with, "Of course it is." But truly grasping and embodying this concept would require learners (and teachers) to make space for failure, to build in opportunities for exploration that might not initially result in success—and to accept their own writing failures with grace and the confidence that this is just part of how writing works. Thus, the idea stated in a concept might seem simple, but restating it is not learning it. Moving through liminality to the point where the learner embodies the concept in how she sees and acts is difficult and might even be a life-long task.

Another possible reaction to reading some of these threshold concepts might be: "What are these people talking about?" There is no amount of defining and re-stating that can help learners truly grasp a concept that might only be learned through experience. For example,

another threshold concept in this book is that writing involves the negotiation of language difference. Depending upon the learner's own experiences, this concept might seem either obvious or completely inexpli-
cable. Learning to understand this concept might require engaging with
other language users who speak different forms of a language, studying theories about language use, and attempting to work with varied
language users in vari s settings—for example, as a tutor in a writing
center or as a new te. er. There is sometimes no amount of "telling"
that can speed up a learner's understanding of a difficult threshold concept. Only experience, assistance from experts in a field, and continued
reflection and struggle can help a learner get through the liminal space.

Our point here is that this classroom edition of *Naming What We Know*
is not a textbook, and the threshold concept summaries found here cannot be expected to do the work of "teaching" newcomers threshold concepts. They might assist in providing some language to talk about difficult ideas, or help in making explicit some often unstated assumptions,
but no reader should expect that reading the concepts outlined in this
book will result in "mastery" of those concepts.

We also will repeat here an admonition that we included in the fuller
text: it is too easy for teachers and administrators to hear about threshold concepts and then immediately attempt to turn them into goals for
a one-quarter or one-semester class, checklist items, or rubric contents.
But threshold concepts do not—and should not—lend themselves to
these kinds of short-term outcomes or assessments. Threshold concepts
represent the deep, transformative, foundational learning of disciplines.
When and how learners come to threshold concepts, and what learners
need in order to really begin to grasp and embody them, is extremely
varied. We cannot expect to see the learning and transformation happen at the end of one assignment or one class or even one or two semes-
ters or quarters. Our role as teachers is to provide space for this deep
learning and to try to explicitly state the underlying assumptions about
our subject matter that are often unstated. Not stating what we know can
easily get in the way of transformational learning. On the other hand,
stating what we know is necessary and helpful, but not sufficient. A lot
of "doing" has to happen as well. We hope that this collection provides
a useful step along that pathway to "doing."

References

Bowker, Geoffrey and Susan Leigh Star. 1999. *Sorting Things Out: Classification and Its Consequences*. Cambridge, MA: MIT Press.

Kreber, Carolin. 2009. "Supporting Student Learning in the Context of Diversity, Complexity, and Uncertainty." In *The University and Its Disciplines: Teaching and Learning Within and Beyond Disciplinary Boundaries*, ed. Carolin Kreber, 3–18. New York: Routledge.

Meyer, Jan H. F. and Ray Land. 2006. "Threshold Concepts and Troublesome Knowledge: An Introduction." In *Overcoming Barriers to Student Learning*, ed. Jan H. F. Meyer and Ray Land, 3–18. London: Routledge.

Introduction

COMING TO TERMS
Composition/Rhetoric, Threshold Concepts, and a Disciplinary Core

Kathleen Blake Yancey

From the modern beginnings of the field of rhetoric and composition, we in the field have shared a self-evident claim about the primary focus of rhetoric and composition: that it has at its center the practice of writing and its teaching. At the same time, this observation, as straightforward as it may seem, begs more than one question. What do we mean by writing? Is it practice, or practices? Is what we are talking about writing, or composing, or both? What concepts can or do we draw upon to theorize writing practices? What of any of this do we share with students, when, and how? Historically, questions such as these, typically using the classroom as the site where they are worked out, have defined the field. In the first issue of *College Composition and Communication*, for example, John Gerber (1950, 12) spoke to this point exactly:

> Someone has estimated that there are at least nine thousand of us teaching in college courses in composition and communication. Faced with many of the same problems, concerned certainly with the same general objectives, we have for the most part gone our separate ways, experimenting here and improvising there. Occasionally we have heard that a new kind of course is working well at Upper A. M. or that a new staff training program has been found successful at Lower T. C. But we rarely get the facts. We have had no systematic way of exchanging views and information quickly. Certainly we have had no means of developing a coordinated research program.

Some fifty-five years later, Richard Fulkerson, delivering in 2005 a third iteration of analysis in a career-long search to trace the field's coherence—he published his first analysis in 1979, the second in 1990—speaks to the situation of the field in the early twenty-first century, and from a Gerberian perspective, it's both good news and bad. On the one hand, we have what Gerber longed for, the scholarship and multiple venues permitting *"a systematic way of exchanging views and information*

DOI: 10.7330/9781607325789.c000a

quickly." On other hand, that very scholarship allows Fulkerson to make a claim not unlike Gerber's: we are not coherent, do not have a core set of beliefs or values.

> Within the scholarship, we currently have three alternative axiologies (theories of value): the newest one, the social or social-construction view, which values critical cultural analysis; an expressive one; and a multifaceted rhetorical one. I maintain that the three axiologies drive the three major approaches to the teaching of composition[:] (1) critical/cultural studies [CCS], (2) expressivism, and (3) procedural rhetoric. (Fulkerson 2005, 655)

What we do have despite our differences, according to Fulkerson, is our teaching of writing process and a commitment to writing pedagogy, even if, as Fulkerson claims, our commitment is really plural; it takes different forms. What seems to be missing, since the beginning of the field and even in this late age of print, is any consensus in the field on what we might call the *content of composition*: the questions, kinds of evidence, and materials that define disciplines and would thus define us as well.[1] Fulkerson's theory is that, at least in the case of CCS, its focus on texts allows for a kind of content that faculty find inherently satisfying and that, in the specific instance of CCS, scholars and teachers in rhetoric and composition value given their backgrounds and their commitments to social justice.

> Both the lit-based course and the cultural studies course reflect, I suspect, content envy on the part of writing teachers. Most of us (still) have been trained in textual analysis: we like classes built around texts to analyze. (And I am certainly not immune to that envy. I *enjoy* leading discussions of complex nonfiction that challenges students to think hard about basic beliefs.) (Fulkerson 2005, 663)

This, then, is the field-specific scene for *Naming What We Know*, which proceeds along very different lines and makes a very different kind of argument than the field has seen previously. As coeditors Linda Adler-Kassner and Elizabeth Wardle explain in the next chapter of this volume, the project has two parts: (1) identifying threshold concepts, in this case thirty-seven of them, providing a core for the field in terms of what we know; and (2) outlining how they can be helpful in various writing-focused and writing-related contexts. To develop the thirty-seven threshold concepts, Adler-Kassner and Wardle invited many scholars to "[look] at the research and theory to determine what they could agree we collectively know" (4). In addition, drawing on these concepts, a subset of these scholars share with us how we might use the concepts in our pedagogical projects and in our extra-classroom work with students and colleagues.

Invitations to contribute to this project, then, provided an occasion to think about the field in the company of colleagues, about what it is we have learned over the last half century, and about what it is we think we now know—about writing and composing, about the features and practices of writing we take as axiomatic, and about the terms that locate and define writing. Put another way, Adler-Kassner and Wardle's invitation functioned as an exigence, an opportunity to uncover and interrogate assumptions; in that sense, identifying the threshold concepts presented here was a collective philosophical exercise involving exploration as much as consolidation of what we know. Moreover, that there *are* such concepts, features, and practices is evidenced by the conceptual map presented in the first part of *Naming*. At the same time, our work, the work of rhetoric and composition located in rhetoric w it large, has historically included a practical component; threshold concepts are helpful in this sphere as well, as we see in the second half of the book, where contributors recount the various ways—in retrospect, in the current moment, and in a future time—that threshold concepts help us engage as teacher-scholars, whether we are teaching first-year composition students, designing a new major, engaging with doctoral students, or working with our colleagues in general education or writing across the curriculum.[2]

***

What do threshold concepts offer composition studies? At first glance, they may seem like a kind of canon, a list of the defining key terms of the discipline, with an explicit emphasis on definition and the implication of dogma. At a second glance, and according to all the writers in part 2 of *Naming*, they seem much more contingent—presented here not as canonical statement, but rather as articulation of shared beliefs providing multiple ways of helping us name what we know and how we can use what we know in the service of writing. That use value, as described in the chapters, takes various forms. In one version, threshold concepts function as boundary objects, allowing us to toggle between the beliefs of the discipline and those of individual institutions; in another version, they function as a heuristic or portal for planning; in yet another version, they seem a set of propositions that can be put into dialogue with threshold concepts from a subdiscipline or from a different discipline for a richly layered map of a given phenomenon. Each of the chapters within shows us how such versions might work.

Heidi Estrem opens the first set of chapters in part 2, "Using Threshold Concepts in Program and Curriculum Design," with her chapter outlining the role threshold concepts have played in general education reform efforts at Boise State University. Writing outcomes, she observes (as do others like Elizabeth Wardle and Blake Scott), are too targeted to the end point, too keyed to a linear trajectory of learning, too decontextualized, and over time too standardized.

> Generalized, outcomes-based depictions of student learning about writing hold two immediate challenges: (1) they locate evidence of writing at the *end* of key experiences—certainly one valuable place to begin understanding learning, but not the only place; and (2) they often depict writing as only a skill (albeit an "intellectual" or at least "practical" one) (AAC&U 2013). While outcomes-based depictions hold a certain kind of currency and explanatory power in educational reform efforts and will likely continue to do so, a threshold concepts approach provides a differently meaningful framework for intervening in commonplace understandings about writing. Threshold concepts offer a mechanism for faculty to articulate the content of thei˙   urses, identify student learning throughout the course experience, a˙.   create shared values for writing in a way that a focus on end products—on outcomes—cannot. (89)

Focusing on upper-level communication in the disciplines (CID) courses, Estrem demonstrates how an approach to writing in the disciplines shaped by the idea of threshold concepts changes the game, in part through highlighting the idea underlying the threshold concepts that writing is a discipline with the discipline hosting the CID and *its* threshold concepts, in part by creating a common framework for the institution locating the CIDs both vertically and horizontally:

> Within our new learning outcomes framework, the communication-in-the-disciplines (CID) courses are both discipline specific (housed in departments, taught by departmental faculty) *and* explicitly linked to the Writing Undergraduate Learning Outcome. In these courses, then, writing is taught not as an isolated skill but as disciplinary practice, an embodiment of "how people 'think' within a discipline" (Meyer and Land 2003, 1). The CID courses are thus a particularly rich site for considering (1) what the threshold concepts for writing *at the introduction to the discipline* might be; (2) how they illuminate or complicate the Writing University Learning Outcome; and (3) how their depiction might begin to foster particular kinds of identification and alliance, both vertically along the Writing Undergraduate Learning Outcome trajectory (how might threshold concepts for writing connect from English 101 and 102, UF 200, CID, and Finishing Foundations?) *and* horizontally, among faculty who teach communication-in-the-disciplines courses across campus (how might these courses with substantially different content and focus foster student writing development in appropriate ways?). (96)

In the second chapter in part 1, Doug Downs and Liane Robertson take up the role of threshold concepts in first-year composition (FYC), which, given the field's recent attention to transfer, seems a timely question. Even without that salience, however, the role threshold concepts might play in FYC is a good question since, by definition, writers *are* nascent members of the field, at least to the extent that they are informed practitioners. What can threshold concepts help us understand about what it means to be informed? Downs and Robertson write in retrospect since they have not used threshold concepts to design curriculum, but they agree that FYC should focus on two aspects of threshold concepts: "To say that FYC will focus on threshold concepts, then, is to say that it will, in part, focus on misconceptions and work toward richer conceptualizations of writing" (105). For purposes of transfer, four areas or categories in FYC are crucial:

> Our experiences have suggested that four areas present particular challenges when we attempt to address FYC's twin missions (addressing misconceptions and teaching for transfer): writing as human interaction (rhetoric); textuality; epistemology (ways of knowing and the nature of knowledge); and writing process. Students' misconceptions about writing most often relate to one of these categories. (107)

The goal of this approach isn't only a change in writing practices or a greater understanding of writing, but, much as Yancey, Robertson and Taczak (2014) argue in *Writing across Contexts: Transfer, Composition, and Sites of Writing*, that students develop their own theory of writing. As Downs and Robertson explain:

> Every writer has a set of knowledges and beliefs about writing, some explicit and some tacit, that make up their personal theory of writing. The conceptions that make up this personal theory are developed through education, experience, observation, and cultural narratives of writing; few writers will ever explicitly articulate their theory, but they will live by it. By *theory*, we mean a systematic narrative of lived experience and observed phenomena that both accounts for (makes sense of) past experience and makes predictions about future experience. The "better"—the more completely, consistently, and elegantly—a theory accounts for past experience, and the more accurate its predictions about future experience, the stronger or more robust it is, and thus the more useful it is. The writer's personal theory of writing—their conceptions of what happens when they write, what ought to be happening, why that does or does not happen—shapes both their actions while writing and their interpretations of the results of their writing activities. This theory of writing and the set of conceptions that make it up are how a writer—in our case, an FYC student—understands "the game" of writing. (110)

In the next chapter, J. Blake Scott and Elizabeth Wardle's account of how threshold concepts can inform the design of a major in rhetoric and composition, we see a plan for students to take up threshold concepts in a more sophisticated way, as is appropriate for a major in the field involving several courses. Scott and Wardle's narrative of their experience at the University of Central Florida raises two sets of questions about the role threshold concepts can play in the design of a major: What are our threshold concepts, assuming we agree there are such concepts, and if named, what assumptions does their naming reveal? and How can they function as a framework for curriculum design?

Like Downs and Robertson, Scott and Wardle did not begin their curricular design process "by directly considering threshold concepts" but rather "have come to believe that doing so could have been a helpful addition to [their] curriculum planning" (123). More specifically, like Estrem, Scott and Wardle see the value of threshold concepts in curricular planning in their use as an adaptive framework, in the "flexible alignment" provided by threshold concepts, in contrast to what they see as the "standardization" of outcomes: "*The nature of threshold concepts —* not goals, not learning outcomes, but foundational assumptions that inform learning across time—makes them *flexible* tools for imagining a progression of student learning across a curriculum rather than at one specific moment or in one short period of time" (123). In creating their design for the major, the writing department at UCF employed multiple frameworks, each of which is keyed to the overarching threshold concept that writing and rhetoric is a subject of study:

> We began by identifying three overlapping strands of the field's scholarship: rhetorical studies, writing studies, and literacy and language studies, the latter including linguistics. We also categorized the field in another way—naming pedagogical, historical, and theoretical scholarship as important overlapping dimensions of the field's work. (124)

Moreover, in drawing on threshold concepts, the UCF group created variations of them through three processes: modification, extension, and boundary marking. Thus, for example, in designing the curriculum, the UCF group was implicitly guided by two related threshold concepts discussed in part 1 of this collection—that Writing Is a Rhetorical and Social Activity (1.0) and that Writing Speaks to Situations through Recognizable Forms (2.0)—along with the premise that *practice adapting writing in various types of contexts is an effective way to improve writing competencies*, a variation of the threshold concept that Learning to Write Effectively Requires Different Kinds of Practice, Time, and Effort (4.3, 126).

Ultimately, the major at UCF will ask students, much like Downs' and Robertson's students, to create their own theory of writing, in this case using an electronic portfolio inside the capstone as the reflective site for this work.

In considering doctoral education in rhetoric and composition, Kara Taczak and I take up another site where threshold concepts are integral: the question is how they might be so.

> More specifically, as this volume explains and illustrates, given that faculty can identify threshold concepts they believe locate the field, it's reasonable to expect we would also see them informing doctoral education given the nature of such education: they introduce students to, and in some ways socialize them into, the field, whether explicitly or more implicitly (142).

Using the Florida State University doctoral program in rhetoric and composition as a site for analysis, Kara and I use three integrated doctoral curricula—the delivered, lived, and experienced curricula—as lenses for inquiry.

> The *delivered form of the curriculum,* which we take up first, is defined . . . as the curriculum "we design. We see it in syllabi, where course goals are articulated. . . . We see it in assignments, where students deal with the specifics of the curriculum. We see it in readings, where students enter a specific discourse and specific ways of thinking" (Yancey 2004, 17). In the case of the FSU doctoral program in writing studies, we would expect to find threshold concepts in courses—in descriptions, syllabi, and assignments—as well as in nonclassroom sites like preliminary exams and the dissertation (142).
>
> The second kind of curriculum, . . . the "lived curriculum," is the set of "prior courses and experiences and connections that contextualize the delivered curriculum" (Yancey 2004, 16) as well as the curriculum into which students will graduate: as our review of the FSU doctoral program in RC shows, its purpose is to prepare students through the delivered curriculum for the lived curriculum of the field.
>
> But of course, students will make their own sense of the curriculum, and that's a third and final curriculum, the *experienced curriculum,* "what some call the de facto curriculum—that is, the curriculum that *students construct* in the context of the delivered curriculum we seek to share" (Yancey 2004, 58). This curriculum, then, is the enactment of the delivered curriculum by the students themselves. (142)

In sum, the three different curricula provide different opportunities to encounter and work with different threshold concepts.

In the context of the other curricula discussed in this volume, one of the more interesting dimensions of this model of education is the kind of opportunity we see for learning inside the lived curriculum, given that "it operates in a context outside of the program and sometimes . . . outside of the academy" (Taczak and Yancey, 146). It's here that "students are more inclined to experience another threshold concept, that of failure" (146), a threshold concept defined by Collin Brooke and Allison Carr:

> As students progress throughout their educational careers and the expec-
> tations for their writing evolve from year to year and sometimes course to
> course, there is no way that we can expect them to be able to intuit these
> shifting conditions. They must have the opportunity to try, to fail, and to
> learn from those failures as a means of intellectual growth. (63)

How to help students learn from *failures as a means of intellectual growth*
is particularly important as graduate students cross the threshold from
doctoral education into faculty positions in the field.

Addressing writing assessment as she opens the second section
of chapters, Enacting Threshold Concepts about Writing across the
University, Peggy O'Neill considers how threshold concepts from two
disciplines contribute to a cross-disciplinary field, in this case the field
of writing assessment, located in assessment and in writing. As O'Neill
explains, neither set of concepts is subordinate to the other; to work
effectively, practitioners need to understand both.

> While writing studies' threshold concepts are central to understand-
> ing writing assessment, they are not sufficient to such understanding
> because writing assessment lies at the intersection of threshold concepts
> specific to writing studies and those specific to educational assessment.
> Understanding writing assessment therefore requires understanding
> both sets of concepts and how they interact. Writing studies profession-
> als who design and administer assessments must learn to understand
> critical concepts of validity and reliability associated with psychometrics
> since these concepts are widely used across disciplines and assessment
> contexts and have established power in the discourse of education and
> assessment. Conversely, assessment specialists, who may be responsible for
> designing and evaluating assessments across a variety of disciplines and
> contexts, must understand the threshold concepts associated with writing
> (articulated in part I) if they are working in writing assessment. Both sets
> of concepts are required to create assessments that produce valid results
> and to use those results effectively and responsibly. (158)

In developing this line of thinking, O'Neill makes two other important points. First, she observes that writing assessment addresses many
situations, from classroom to program. Second, she points out that it's
through tapping the interdisciplinary threshold concepts that we can
develop new practices and make new knowledge.

Rebecca S. Nowacek and Bradley Hughes take up the question of
how threshold concepts might enhance the tutoring of writing, focusing
on three areas: writing-tutor education, writing-tutor practice, and the
development of threshold concepts at the intersection of writing studies
and tutoring. Nowacek, for example, raises the issue of priorities as a way
of deciding what to include in a course preparing students to tutor, and,
like many of the chapter authors, she begins with questions.

The notion of threshold concepts implies that writing tutors will be better equipped for their work if they learn to see with and through the threshold concepts of writing. If that is the case, how should a tutor-education program sequence the work of grappling with those threshold concepts? Are some threshold concepts more central to writing center work than others? Asking these TC-inspired questions has helped [me] better understand three dimensions of the tutor education program at Marquette: choosing what to prioritize during the initial tutor-education course and what to defer until ongoing tutor education, making clearer decisions about hiring processes, and revising the content of the tutor-education course. (174)

As important, once fully engaged in writing center practice, tutors may find threshold concepts useful in understanding practice, especially that occurring within the less successful tutorial; as Nowacek and Hughes put it, threshold concepts can be helpful in "illuminating possible explanations for writers' resistance" (178). Last but not least and perhaps most intriguing, they propose the category of writing center-specific threshold concepts. As an illustration, they nominate "tutors need to learn that *experienced, effective conversational partners for writers regularly inhabit the role of 'expert outsider,'* and tutors need to learn the skills necessary for inhabiting that role" (181). Here, then, the role of expert outsider is identified as a rhetorical situation through which practice can be understood.

Linda Adler-Kassner and John Majewski take up another issue, the role threshold concepts can play "in the service of professional development." Borrowing Jan H. F. Meyer's trajectory of faculty engagement, Adler-Kassner and Majewski add two other frameworks for a robust approach:

The trajectory [of professional development] includes four phases: (1) describing threshold concepts of their discipline; (2) using threshold concepts as an "interpretive framework" through which to consider teaching; (3) reflexively incorporating them into teaching practices; and (4) conducting research on teaching and understanding teaching as research (Meyer 2012, 11). Meyer's study echoes elements of other literature focusing on professional development, such as Middendorf and Pace's (2004) Decoding the Disciplines (DtD) process, which leads faculty through a seven-step process beginning with identification of "learning bottlenecks" (points where students get stuck in a course), which leads to an examination of expert knowledge related to the bottleneck, finally resulting in the design and assessment of pedagogical activities that address the sticking point (decodingthedisciplines.org). In the frameworks of both Meyer and Joan Middendorf and David Pace, teaching is intimately connected to creative application of expert knowledge in a manner similar to academic research. As Sarah Bunnell and Daniel

Bernstein argue, the application of this knowledge (here, represented in threshold concepts) to teaching is a "scholarly enterprise" that includes understanding teaching as an "active, inquiry-based process" and seeing teaching as a "public act contributing to 'community property'" that leads to "open dialogue about teaching questions and student work." (Meyer 2012, 15; 186)

At the heart of this approach are two kinds of expertise: first, threshold concepts in the discipline; and second, "expertise associated with knowledge about how to learn and represent threshold concepts" (Adler-Kassner and Majewski, 187).

Professional development, of course, is predicated on the idea that something will change; as Adler-Kassner and Majewski put it, "A key question is how an introduction to threshold concepts [can] change actual teaching practice" (196). More specifically, focusing on Majewski's general education class in history, the coauthors point to the role of explicitness as critical for such change, the ways it can highlight disciplinarity, and how, working together, the two can assist learners:

> More emphasis was ˌ ˑ on teaching skills specific to a history course, such as reading primary sources or connecting historical evidence to arguments. To illustrate the way historians read and the importance of identifying context, for instance, students viewed a video of a think-aloud exercise in which John struggled to interpret a primary source document from ancient Rome. In a similar fashion, students were instructed in lecture on specific ways historians craft arguments, especially how to approach an analytical thesis and how to directly link evidence to argument. The necessity of having a meaningful argument was repeatedly emphasized—to write history, students could not just summarize facts but had to interpret facts in ways that made them significant. To do so, they had to write analytical narratives that flowed chronologically but still made an overall argument. The course thus explicitly reminded students that their analytical narratives were particular to the threshold concepts of history and reinforced these concepts through lecture and hands-on activity. They were writing in a particular context that would develop a different set of skills than would courses in other disciplines. (198)

In the final chapter, Chris Anson considers how writing as it occurs across a campus can be enhanced through the use of threshold concepts. Defining writing as a disciplinary activity, Anson explains the role that six threshold concepts can play in this work:

- defining writing as a disciplinary activity;
- reconceptualizing the social and rhetorical nature of writing;
- distinguishing between writing to learn and writing to communicate;

- establishing shared goals and responsibilities for improvement;
- understanding the situated nature of writing and the problem of transfer; and
- viewing student writing developmentally. (205)

As important, Anson points out how important it is to work with threshold concepts in what we might call their *fullness*. When we don't, when for example "threshold concepts are reduced from verbs to nouns, from their fully articulated, active form (along with plentiful explanation) to buzzwords and catch phrases, many faculty will balk, and resistance can follow" (216). As a corrective to this, Anson notes the relationship of a single maxim to a full set of threshold concepts. Much as we see in the explanation of the threshold concepts in the first part of *Naming What We Know*, each one is in relation to several others; to understand it, we have to understand it in the context of the others.

> During some campus visits, my hosts have counseled me never to use a specific word among the faculty, such as *outcomes* or *rubric* or even *WAC*, usually because some earlier curricular disaster or failed innovation poisoned the entire campus to whatever the term meant at the time. Although it is less likely, certain threshold concepts introduced too glibly can trigger false assumptions, resistance, or confusion among faculty. An example familiar to most WAC leaders takes the problematically reduced form of advice not to focus first (or even at all) on the surface features of students' writing: "students' grammatical mistakes are not as important as what they are trying to say" or even "don't focus on grammar." Unpacking this assertion means delving into the relationship between form and meaning, the effects of certain pedagogies on students' self-efficacy and further writing behaviors, the relationship among writing assignments and learning goals, students' linguistic backgrounds, and a host of other complicated issues. (216)

***

Reading across these chapters, we can see eight points of agreement.

First, we agree on the metaconcept that writing is an activity and a subject of study. This threshold concept thus expands the field's historical focus on practice to include writing as a subject of study as well. For some colleagues, as Blake Scott and Elizabeth Wardle suggest, this is a provocative claim; not all faculty agree that there are threshold concepts in the field, much less agree on what they might be. At the same time, what we also see in the claim that writing is a subject of study is that writing has a content, a claim that the rest of the threshold concepts detail. If this is so, we need have Fulkerson's content envy no longer.

Second, we agree that a threshold concept functions as both propositional statement and heuristic for inquiry, a heuristic we can, in

Heidi Estrem's terms, see with and through. Their value as propositions is twofold: we articulate what we know, and we can use that articulation as a point of departure for additional scholarly investigation.

Third, we agree that threshold concepts provide a way of thinking, a framework for multiple kinds of work, be it the design of general education or the foundational principles for writing across the curriculum.

Fourth, we agree that threshold concepts aren't fixed but are rather contingent and flexible, and that to be helpful, they need to be so. Entailed in this agreement is a sense that outcomes, which have offered both promise and help to writing programs, have become rigid and standardized; as such, they provide a foil to threshold concepts.

Fifth, we agree that threshold concepts are neither acontextual nor arhetorical, but are specific to a discipline and community of practice; they often function as a kind of boundary object in dialogue with local situations and/or other frameworks, including those connected to the discipline, as in Downs and Robertson's design for FYC, and to other fields, as we see in O'Neill's discussion of writing assessment.

Sixth, we agree, as Scott and Wardle and Nowacek and Hughes illustrate, that as threshold concepts are employed in a given setting, variants of the threshold concepts can develop, ones that themselves toggle between more general threshold concepts and understandings informing the local.

Seven, we agree, as Adler-Kassner and Majewski argue, that we need to be explicit in working with both faculty and students, and that such explicitness, as explained in *How People Learn*, facilitates transfer.

And eighth, we agree that all of us—including students—can use threshold concepts to inquire, analyze, interpret, and, ultimately, make knowledge.

***

We have long been interested in mapping our field. In 1984, for example, Janice Lauer took up that task, beginning by identifying the core features of a discipline to contextualize her argument that at that time, rhetoric and composition was an emerging discipline.

> At its deepest level, a discipline has a special set of phenomena to study, a characteristic mode or modes of inquiry, its own history of development, its theoretical ancestors and assumptions, its evolving body of knowledge, and its own epistemic courts by which knowledge gains that status. (Lauer 1984, 20)

Some twenty years later, then-*CCC Online* editor Collin Brooke employed databases and linking to create another kind of map; and nearly ten years after that, Derek Mueller (2012) plotted the long tail of composition, and graduate students at CUNY began sharing their academic genealogy project. The exploration into threshold concepts and their uses presented in this volume provides yet another approach to the field's larger mapping project, here a process identifying not only the map, but also *what* there is to map. In this sense, threshold concepts are kairotic: they articulate the substance of the field as a mechanism for mapping the field itself.

It may also be that threshold concepts, as presented here, mark another kind of threshold for the field, an idea that's occurred to me as I've participated in articulating key concepts, in providing definitions for two of the threshold concepts, in coauthoring a chapter, in reading this volume, and in writing this introduction. In reviewing the list of contributors to threshold concepts, for example, I was interested in the timeline we might draw, collectively accounting for their scholarly contributions. A back-of-the-envelope calculation might begin with Andrea Lunsford's "Classical Rhetoric and Technical Writing," published in a 1976 issue of *College Composition and Communication*, and continue through the 2015 publication of this volume: that's nearly forty years of a sixty-five year history of the discipline.

But my review of the list of chapter authors prompted another insight, in part because I had just read Robert Connors's observations about "generations" of "modern composition specialists": he dates the first generation as occurring between the "late 1940s and the early 1960s" and the second occurring in the 1960s into the 1970s, and he notes that the specialists of both these generations "retool[ed] as writing specialists after literary doctorates" (Connors 1999, 9). The third generation—and he counts himself in that generation—took their doctorates in rhetoric and composition at a limited number of institutions,[3] and Connors cites this generation as something of a dividing line, in the development of the field, between those who retooled to found a field and those who entered a field already in progress. I'm not sure precisely how I would date the generations, but there's no doubt that early leaders of the field took their doctoral work in literature and English education;[4] and there's no doubt that these early leaders—and leaders in some of the succeeding generations as well—were attracted to the field in large part because it wasn't established and they thus could make significant contributions to what they saw as an emerging field (Craig et al. forthcoming). The assumption underlying *Naming*, of course, is that the field *is* now established, and it thus would be a useful enterprise to consider together what it is that we do know. This established field, of course, is the field that most of the chapter contributors entered: teacher-scholars who saw not only an established field, but a field so established that it includes defined subfields—among them writing centers, writing assessment, and WAC—often providing their own pathways into the larger field; who chose graduate study in rhetoric and composition from one of more than eighty institutions currently offering the doctorate in rhetoric and composition; and whose education was not necessarily taken in English departments nor, even when it was, defined by literature. It occurred to me, in other words, that the literary context so prominent in so many accounts of our history and even in accounts of our pedagogy, as Fulkerson explains, is, for these contributors, as for new generations, no longer our default context—or, and at least as important, our default *content*. And it also occurred to me that our shared interest in threshold concepts, which is an expression of an interest in disciplinarity, is a logical next step when a field has matured, as ours has.

If this is so, then by means of this project, we are entering another threshold for the field, one with enormous potential to help shape the field's future.

Notes

1. The field has intermittently taken up the question of the content of composition, most recently in 2006 and sponsored by the CCCC, though it was quite clear that not everyone agreed that there is such a content. For a summary of the CCCC-sponsored discussion, see http://compfaqs.org/ContentofComposition/HomePage.

2. It's worth noting that taken together, the chapters address the full set of responsibilities a faculty member in the discipline of rhetoric and composition might take up, including the one program that has now completed the set, the major in rhetoric and composition. In 1999, Robert Connors made the argument that to coalesce as a discipline, composition needed two "elements": "methods of intellectual tradition in a great burgeoning of journals and books" and a "method of scholarly reproduction" (Connors 1999, 8), by which he meant doctoral programming. In 2004, I argued that for the field to become a discipline, another element was needed, the major in rhetoric and composition: "In other words, it is past time that we fill the glaringly empty spot between first-year composition and graduate education with a composition major" (Yancey 2004, 308).

3. There were several other programs predating the ones on Connors's list, including the well-known doctoral program at the University of Iowa.

4. See, for example, Stock's 2011 edited *Composition's Roots in English Education*.

References

Connors, Robert. 1999. "Composition History and Disciplinarity." In *History, Reflection, and Narrative: The Professionalism of Composition*, edited by Debra Journet, Beth Boehm, and Mary Rosner, 1963–1983: 3–23. Stanford, CA: Ablex.

Craig, Jacob, Matt Davis, Christine Martorana, Josh Mehler, Kendra Mitchell, Antony N. Ricks, Bret Zawilski, and Kathleen Blake Yancey. Forthcoming. "Against the Rhetoric and Composition Grain: A Microhistorical View." In *Microhistories of Composition*, edited by Bruce McComiskey. Logan: Utah State University Press.

Fulkerson, Richard. 2005. "Composition at the Turn of the Twenty-First Century." *College Composition and Communication* 56 (4): 654–87.

Gerber, John. 1950. "The Conference on College Composition and Communication." *College Composition and Communication* 1 (1):12.

Lauer, Janice. 1984. "Composition Studies: Dappled Discipline." *Rhetoric Review* 3 (1): 20–29. http://dx.doi.org/10.1080/07350198409359074.

Meyer, Jan H. F. 2012. "Variation in Student Learning as a Threshold Concept." *Journal of Faculty Development* 26 (3): 9–13.

Meyer, Jan H. F., and Ray Land. 2003. "Threshold Concepts and Troublesome Knowledge: Linkages to Ways of Thinking and Practising." ETL Project Occasional Report 4. http://www.etl.tla.ed.ac.uk/docs/ETLreport4.pdf.

Mueller, Derek. 2012. "Grasping Rhetoric and Composition by Its Long Tail: What Graphs Can Tell Us about the Field's Changing Shape." *College Composition and Communication* 64 (1): 195–223.

Stock, Patricia, ed. 2011. *Composition's Roots in English Education*. Portsmouth, NH: Heineman.

Yancey, Kathleen Blake. 2004. "Made Not Only in Words: Composition in a New Key." *College Composition and Communication* 56 (2): 297–328. http://dx.doi.org/10.2307/4140651.

Yancey, Kathleen Blake, Liane Robertson, and Kara Taczak. 2014. *Writing Across Contexts: Transfer, Composition, and Sites of Writing*. Logan: Utah State University Press.

NAMING WHAT WE KNOW

NAMING WHAT WE KNOW
The Project of This Book

Linda Adler-Kassner and Elizabeth Wardle

Reading across the last fifty years of research, it is possible to make a case that our field has in many ways been concerned with its constitution *as* field. Researchers and teachers have reflected on what the field is, whether it is a field, and so on—and on a fairly regular basis. That these are fraught questions is evident in our difficulty even settling on a name for the field. Within the last ten or so years, we seem to have settled on three terms—*composition, rhetoric,* and *writing studies,* individually or in combination with one another—to speak to the collective efforts of the discipline.

But while we have engaged in what James Carey, perhaps slightly misquoting John Dewey, refers to as "the neurotic quest for certainty" (Carey 1989, 89) in pursuit of these questions about the external boundaries of the field, researchers and teachers *in* the field have, at the same time, focused on questions related to a common theme: *the study of composed knowledge.* Within this theme, our work has been expansive. To name just a few areas of practice within it, we have studied what composed knowledge looks like in specific contexts; how good and less-than-good qualities of composed knowledge are defined, by whom, and with what values associated with those definitions and qualities; how to help learners compose knowledge within specific contexts and with what consequences for learner and context; the relationships between technologies and processes for composing knowledge; connections between affordances and potential for composing knowledge; and how composed knowledge can be best assessed and why.

As we have taken on these questions associated with composed knowledge, writing researchers, instructors, and programs have simultaneously attempted to participate in discussions—with one another and with others (such as departmental colleagues, administrators, parents,

DOI: 10.7330/9781607325789.c000b

and policymakers)—about what students should learn about writing, how they should learn those things, and how those things should be taught and assessed. These responses have taken two forms. One involves drafting concise, usable statements about best practices extending from the field's knowledge that are intended to be used for policy and practice. This perspective is represented by documents like *The Framework for Success in Postsecondary Writing* or the CCCC *Position Statement on Dual Credit/Concurrent Enrollment Composition: Policy and Best Practices.* Another involves attempts to identify and clarify the boundaries of the discipline as a way of containing, instantiating, and reifying types of writing-related knowledge (e.g., Bizzell 1986; Cook 2011; Kopelsen 2008; Phelps, Wiley, and Gleason 1995; Worsham 1999a, 1999b).

These efforts to outline best practices and outline and clarify the field's boundaries are important. But they sidestep a pressing point: whatever we call ourselves, wherever we may be on the continuum of disciplinarity, fifty (plus) years of research has led us to know some things about the subject of composed knowledge and the questions we ask related to this broad term. This book represents an effort to bring together those things we know using a particular frame, that of threshold concepts.

Threshold concepts are concepts critical for continued learning and participation in an area or within a community of practice. This lens of threshold concepts emerged from a research project in the United Kingdom on the characteristics of effective teaching and learning environments in undergraduate education (Cousin 2006). Jan H. F. Meyer and Ray Land began by studying concepts economists felt were central to the study of their discipline; this lens has now been effectively used to consider threshold knowledge in many other discipline. According to Meyer and Land, threshold concepts have several common characteristics:

- Learning them is generally transformative, involving "an ontological as well as a conceptual shift . . . becoming a part of who we are, how we see, and how we feel" (Cousin 2006).

- Once understood, they are often irreversible and the learner is unlikely to forget them.

- They are integrative, demonstrating how phenomena are related, and helping learners make connections.

- They tend to involve forms of troublesome knowledge, what Perkins refers to as knowledge that is "alien" or counterintuitive (qtd. in Meyer and Land 2006, 3).

While much of the discussion about threshold concepts has been related to how people learn and participate in specific disciplinary communities, threshold concepts of writing studies speak both to and beyond our disciplinary community. This is because the subject of our discipline—composed knowledge—is widely relevant. Consider the ubiquity of some of the field's most widely examined questions: How is "good" composed knowledge (and its opposite) defined? How are students taught to produce composed knowledge? How is composed knowledge assessed? What values are associated with judgments about composed knowledge? and What consequences are attached to the teaching, production, and/or assessment of composed knowledge? Certainly, then, there are threshold concepts of writing studies that are central to participation in the discipline of writing studies; but there are also threshold concepts *from* writing studies that can assist writers and teachers of all sorts, whatever their disciplinary or professional affiliations. The concepts named in this portion of the collection, then, can be positioned differently for different audiences—a first-year writing course, a graduate class, a conversation about writing with a colleague from another department or an administrator, a discussion about writing with a stakeholder outside of the academy. The threshold concepts here also might be considered relevant for audiences inside and beyond the discipline. In this way, both the concepts and our discussions of them in this book differ somewhat from some of the threshold concepts literature that has preceded it, which has been directed almost exclusively toward a disciplinary audience. It also differs from literature in writing studies focusing on reflexive practice, which has been concerned primarily with how to help writers foster a more thorough understanding of their own processes.

COMPOSING PART 1: HOW WE NAMED WHAT WE KNOW

Part 1 of *Naming What We Know* is intended to serve as a sort of crowd-sourced encyclopedia of threshold concepts of writing studies. Any attempt to name what a field knows must be a project taken up by numerous members of the field, and that is what we attempted to elicit with this project. We first identified a group of prominent writing researchers and teachers whose scholarship we believed had made important contributions to the field in a variety of areas, from genre studies to digital composing, from assessment to considerations of identity and diversity in composing. We invited forty-five of those teacher-scholars to participate on a wiki (PBWiki, to which we are enormously grateful for their easy-to-use and stable platform), proposing ideas, phenomena, knowledge, or orientations they considered to be threshold concepts of writing studies. Over several months, twenty-nine of the original forty-five invited participants read the introduction to *Overcoming Barriers to Student Understanding* by Meyer and Land (2006), made fifty-one suggestions regarding what they considered to be threshold concepts, and wrote 139 comments regarding the concepts proposed by others. The two of us then met and analyzed the wiki contributions. We distilled one metaconcept, Writing Is an Activity and a Subject of Study, and five overarching concepts that each seemed to unfold into somewhere between three and nine constituent elements. We circulated this draft among the participants, and after their revisions and approval, we assigned contributors to write extended definitions (one-thousand-word definitions for overarching concepts and five-hundred-word definitions for the subconcepts). Some of these authors took on coauthors at this stage who had not participated in previous stages but who were experts in the concept at hand. Resulting drafts were revised and posted to the wiki. Several concepts were revised, moved, integrated with others, or deleted altogether before the current concepts and categories were finalized. In the end, the members of the group who engaged in this process have identified a total of thirty-seven threshold concepts as "what we know"—from research in writing studies and aligned fields (i.e., linguistics, learning theory, and psychology).

The communities of practice/threshold concepts approach used here is predicated upon the idea that within a community of practice (see Wenger 1999) there is sufficient consensus around these shared ideas; that our writing studies community of practice existed at all was a sort of hypothesis that was tested during the online discussion that led to the developmer of this section of *Naming What We Know*. To this end, rather than begi. ing by attempting to outline the boundaries of the field or speak to particular issues, the participants set about looking at the research and theory to determine what they could agree we collectively know. In this regard, this process parallels Bob Broad's idea of "dynamic criteria mapping" to some extent, an "organic" (Broad 2003) attempt to work from the inside out rather than the other way around. And these efforts led to a surprising amount of agreement.

In the end, both of us—along with the twenty-nine contributors to the wiki—are comfortable identifying these as final-for-now definitions of *some* of what our field knows. But we want to stress the contingent changing nature of knowledge. As a group, we've come to some consensus about some of what we know and agree on at this time in our field's history and development. The concepts and definitions here represent what we know for now; their existence as known concepts is currently critical for epistemological participation in our disciplines, and many of them are, we think, critical for anyone who wants to help learners write more effectively, whatever their disciplines or professions may be. That this knowledge will continue to change, and that what we see as most important will continue to evolve, is inevitable and desirable if we are to continue to grow as a field.

WHY WE NAMED WHAT WE KNOW—
AND NEED TO KEEP DOING SO

Perhaps the value of stopping to name what we know is obvious, but we anticipate that these efforts to have done so will be contentious. Thus, it seems worth taking a little space here to explicitly argue for the need to have engaged in this project, and for the need to continue to engage in it in the coming decades.

There are a number of individuals and groups asserting definitions of what "good writing" is and how it should be developed in schools; this is nothing new. From *Why Johnny Can't Read* (Flesch 1955), published in 1955, to "Why Johnny Can't Write" (Sheils 1975) published in 1975, to *A Nation at Risk* (National Commission on Excellence in Education 1983) in 1983, to the report of the Spellings Commission on the Future of Higher Education that appeared in 2006 (Miller 2006), literacy instruction has long been the subject of scrutiny. What *is* new, though, is the combination of message, funding, and power shared among those involved in this latest round of discussions (see, for instance, Hall and Thomas 2012; Strauss 2013). From this vantage point, then, naming what we know seems particularly important. Broadly, we see a push to standardize ideas about what "good writing" means, extending from what we think of as the college and career readiness agenda. While the Common Core State Standards (2013) (with their focus on three text types: argumentative writing, informative/explanatory writing, and narrative writing) are the most visible evidence of this agenda, the push for writing curricula (and assessments) at the postsecondary level that do not necessarily reflect writing studies research (or the experience of its practitioners) are being felt by some writing faculty in states where legislatures have more control over curricular guidelines, as in Florida, and are hovering just beyond in many other states (such as New York, where the CUNY and SUNY systems have signed an agreement to use Common Core assessments as part of their placement mechanism for students). As both of us (Adler-Kassner 2012; 2014; Downs and Wardle 2007; Wardle 2009; 2012) and others (Applebee 2013; Hesse 2012) have noted, these efforts do *not* always consistently reflect what we know.

In the current educational and policy climate, then, writing carries a heavy burden. It continues both to serve as a vehicle through which knowledge is both generated and demonstrated and to draw the attention of many stakeholders who, regardless of their expertise, weigh in on what "good writing" is, how it should be taught and learned and by whom, and how that learning should be assessed. We hope this effort to begin naming *what we know*—what research about writing, writers, and the act of inscribing knowledge can tell us about fostering knowledge about writing and writing performance that is (still) critical for writers. We also hope this collection can provide a basis for writing studies professionals to describe what we know in ways that are accessible to educated readers (and listeners) who are not necessarily specialists in our discipline. As, however, with any communication between expert practitioners (like writing researchers and teachers) and those with less experienced-based expertise, that communication may take some translating and reframing. For instance, the threshold concept that Habituated Practice Can Lead to Entrenchment (5.3) holds a great deal of meaning to experts, but that meaning is gleaned from deep understandings of the nature of genre, prior knowledge, and identity (as in concepts 2.2, 3.2, and 3.3). We offer the following as a few examples of what this translation or reframing for nonexperts might look like:

Table 0.1

Habituated Practice Can Lead to Entrenchment (5.3).	"Good writing" looks different in different contexts. If writers learn to write one thing or in one way, and they practice just that one thing or way over and over, they might think all writing is like the writing they do, and they might not recognize that good writing looks different and happens differently across different contexts.
Disciplinary and Professional Identities Are Constructed through Writing (3.4).	Faculty use writing (mostly in the form of publications) to share ideas with others and demonstrate that they understand both the ideas of others (research and current issues) and appropriate ways of talking about those ideas in their disciplines. As students delve more deeply into disciplines (as they move, for instance, toward majors or advanced degrees), they are expected to use writing in the ways members of their disciplines do, to engage with others in their disciplinary communities in ways that demonstrate that they understand the work these people do and how to communicate with them, as one of them.

continued on next page

Table 0.1—*continued*

Failure Can Be an Important Part of Writing Development (4.2).	Sometimes, learning what does not work and why it doesn't work can help writers grow, learn, and write more effectively the next time. Learning is not always a process of sequentially mastering skills but is sometimes a messy process that requires revisiting something and having to try again.

The explanations of the threshold concepts in this book are specifically designed to help readers think through what the concepts mean and what their consequences are. They are designed to assist people in the field in explaining them to others. We urge readers to consider how they can best use this content when and if they draw on it for conversations with those outside of our field.

Ultimately, then, the argument here is that our field knows a lot about its subject of study. We know much about how writers write and learn to write, and how best to assess writing. Yet we continue to lose the battle over discussions of writing to stakeholders who have money, power, and influence but little related expertise. If we want to actively and positively impact the lives of writers and writing teachers, we must do a better job of clearly stating what our field knows and helping others understand how to use that knowledge as they set policy, create programs, design and fund assessments, and so on.

UNDERSTANDING AND USING *NAMING WHAT WE KNOW*

We offer this book as a step toward the goal of clearly stating what we know and bring to the table. The collection has two parts. The first is a sort of "encyclopedia" of thirty-seven of the field's threshold concepts arranged in five categories, all of which fall under the metaconcept Writing Is an Activity and a Subject of Study. The second focuses on threshold concepts in action in eight specific sites of writing instruction and writing development. Throughout the book, readers will find references to concepts in the first part of the collection (e.g., 1.4, 3.1, 4.2). These are, in essence, two-dimensional hyperlinks, referencing readers to other, related threshold concepts they might want to think about in relationship to the one about which they are currently reading. If these cross-references become distracting, we urge readers to skip over them or return to them later.

While there are many productive reasons to name what we know, several caveats and cautions are in order regarding how to understand and use the work in this book. First, we want to reiterate that the threshold concepts in this book do not and cannot represent the full set of threshold concepts for our field; in fact, we do not believe it is possible or desirable to try to name, once and for all, all such concepts. Even as we were finalizing categories and threshold concepts after months of dialogue and debate, contributors were noting concepts and indeed entire areas of study they thought had been elided, given short shrift, or left out entirely. We offer these thirty-seven concepts as an effort to begin to name what we know and to invite readers to continue this effort at their own institutions and at conferences and in journals.

Second, these threshold concepts should in no way, shape, or form be used as a checklist—for the development of curriculum, for instance, or to check students' learning. As Kathleen Blake Yancey explains in concept 3.2, Writers' Histories, Processes, and Identities Vary, there has historically been a desire to make "the teaching of writing uniform—mapped across grade levels . . . [in the hopes that] a single approach would enfranchise all writers" (53). There is a difference between naming and describing principles and practices that extend from the research base of a discipline, as this book begins to do, and stripping the complexity from those principles in order to distill them into convenient categories to which generic attributes can be associated or attached. Any attempt to create a "learning checklist" with these (or any other) threshold concepts would, in fact, engage in this complexity stripping (see Land and Meyer 2010 for their discussion of the dangers of "assessment regimes" for the use of threshold concepts).

Heidi Estrem's chapter in part 2 of this collection takes up the more complicated relationship between threshold concepts and learning outcomes, an intersection that also raises questions about the nature of these two ideas. One reason it is not appropriate to conflate learning outcomes and threshold concepts is that threshold concepts are liminal, and learning them happens over time at varied levels of understanding. They often cannot be taught directly by explication but must be experienced and enacted over time with others before they are fully understood. In other words, we cannot expect that students in a single class—first-year composition, for example—would master the threshold concepts outlined in this book. They might be introduced to some of these concepts, they might encounter them, they most certainly will engage in practices that assume some of these threshold concepts to be true. But they will not and cannot be expected to master threshold concepts in a single term or class, and there is no assessment mechanism that can determine whether they have productively encountered them. Learning threshold concepts amounts to learning some of the assumptions of a community of practice, and that only productively happens across time. This type of learning is messy, time consuming, and unpredictable. It does not lend itself to shortcuts or checklists or competency tests.

Rather than become concerned with creating threshold concepts assessments or stripped-down threshold concepts checklists, teachers might more productively consider which threshold concepts inform (or should inform) their classes—particularly looking at sets of classes across time—and whether their curricula and activities are productively acting out of and introducing students to those threshold concepts. In other words, rather than construct a threshold concepts curriculum or a threshold concepts-assessment, readers might consider how these threshold concepts *inform* curriculum or assessment. How, for instance, might the idea that Writing Is an Activity and a Subject of Study contribute to the development of a writing class? What might it look like when learners at multiple levels understand writing as both of these things? Readers might ask themselves whether the writing assessments they are designing act out of generally agreed-upon writing studies threshold concepts, such as Writing Mediates Activity or Writing Is a Way of Enacting Disciplinarity, or whether they are unintentionally enacting harmful conceptions of writing, such as writing is only scribal skills or any piece of writing can be effectively assessed out of context.

In sum, while this book is an effort to name what we know to ourselves and to students and faculty new to our discipline, it is also an effort and a call to extend discussions about what we know to audiences beyond ourselves. As we stressed earlier here, *who* we are and what we call ourselves is less important than *what we know* and the impact that knowledge has. Advocating for writers and writing and making change through knowledge are what matters. We hope this collection proves a productive mechanism for enacting change in writing classrooms, assessments, and policy-writing sessions around the country.

References

Adler-Kassner, Linda. 2012. "The Companies We Keep *or* The Companies We Would Like to Keep: Strategies and Tactics in Challenging Times." *WPA Journal* 36: 119–40.

Adler-Kassner, Linda. (Forthcoming). "Liberal Learning, Professional Training, and Disciplinarity in the Age of Education 'Reform': Remodeling General Education." *College English.*

Applebee, Arthur. 2013. "Common Core State Standards: The Promise and the Peril in a National Palimpsest." *English Journal* 103 (1): 25–33.

Bizzell, Patricia. 1986. "On the Possibility of a Unified Theory of Composition and Literature." *Rhetoric Review* 4 (2): 174–80. http://dx.doi.org/10.1080/073501986093 59121.

Bransford, John D., James W. Pellegrino, and M. Suzanne Donovan, eds. 2000. *How People Learn: Brain, Mind, Experience, and School: Expanded Edition.* Washington, DC: National Academies Press.

Broad, Bob. 2003. *What We Really Value: Beyond Rubrics in Teaching and Assessing Writing.* Logan: Utah State University Press.

Carey, James. 1989. Communication as Culture: Essays on Media and Society. Boston: Unwin and Hyman.

Common Core State Standards. 2013. http://www.corestandards.org/.

Cook, Paul. 2011. "Disciplinarity, Identity Crises, and the Teaching of Writing." In *Who Speaks for Writing?* edited by Ethna D. Lay and Jennifer Rich, 87–102. New York: Peter Lang.

Cousin, Glynis. 2006. "An Introduction to Threshold Concepts." *Planet* 17 (December): 4–5. http://dx.doi.org/10.11120/plan.2006.00170004.

Downs, Doug, and Elizabeth Wardle. 2007. "Teaching about Writing, Righting Misconceptions: (Re)Envisioning FYC as Intro to Writing Studies." *College Composition and Communication* 58 (4): 552–84.

Flesch, Rudolph. 1955. *Why Johnny Can't Read.* New York: Harper & Row.

Fulkerson, Richard. 1990. "Composition in the Eighties." *College Composition and Communication* 41 (4): 409–29. http://dx.doi.org/10.2307/357931.

Hall, Cassie, and Scott L. Thomas. 2012. "'Advocacy Philanthropy' and the Public Policy Agenda: The Role of Modern Foundations in American Higher Education." Paper prepared for the 93rd annual meeting of the American Educational Research Association, Vancouver, Canada.

Hesse, Doug. 2012. "Who Speaks for Writing? Expertise, Ownership, and Stewardship." In *Who Speaks for Writing: Stewardship for Writing Studies in the 21st Century,* edited by Jennifer Rich and Ethna D. Lay, 9–22. New York: Peter Lang.

Kopelson, Karen. 2008. "Sp(l)itting Images; or, Back to the Future of (Rhetoric and?) Composition." *College Composition and Communication* 59 (4): 750–80.

Land, Ray, and Jan H. F. Meyer. 2010. "Threshold Concepts and Troublesome Knowledge (5): Dynamics of Assessment." In *Threshold Concepts and Transformational Learning,* edited by Jan H. F. Meyer, Ray Land, and Caroline Baillie, 61–79. Amsterdam: Sense.

Meyer, Jan H. F., and Ray Land. 2006. "Threshold Concepts and Troublesome Knowledge: An Introduction." In *Overcoming Barriers to Student Understanding,* edited by Jan H. F. Meyer and Ray Land, 3–18. London: Routledge.

Miller, Charles, et al. 2006. *Report of the Commission on the Future of Higher Education.* Washington, DC: US Department of Education.

National Commission on Excellence in Education. 1983. *A Nation at Risk.* Washington, DC: US Department of Education.

Phelps, Louise Wetherbee, Mark Wiley, and Barbara Gleason, eds. 1995. *Composition in Four Keys: Inquiring into the Field.* New York: McGraw-Hill.

Sheils, Merrill. 1975. "Why Johnny Can't Write." *Newsweek*, December 8, 58–65.

Strauss, Valerie. 2013. "Gates Gives 150 Million in Grants for Common Core Standards." *Answer Sheet* (blog), May 12. http://www.washingtonpost.com/blogs/answer-sheet/wp/2013/05/12/gates-gives-150-million-in-grants-for-common-core-standards/.

Wardle, Elizabeth. 2009. "   t Genres' and the Goal of FYC: How Can We Help Students Write the Gen   of the University?" *College Composition and Communication* 60 (4): 765–88.

Wardle, Elizabeth. 2012. "Creative Repurposing for Expansive Learning: Considering 'Problem-Exploring' and 'Answer-Getting' Dispositions in Individuals and Fields." *Composition Forum* 26. http://compositionforum.com/issue/26/creative-repurposing.php.

Wenger, Etienne. 1999. *Communities of Practice: Learning, Meaning, and Identity.*

Cambridge: Cambridge University Press.

Worsham, Lynn. 1999a. "Critical Interference and the Postmodern Turn in Composition Studies." *Composition Forum* 10: 1–29.

Worsham, Lynn. 1999b. "On the Rhetoric of Theory in the Discipline of Writing: A Comment and a Proposal." *JAC: A Journal of Rhetoric.* 19: 389–409.

Threshold Concepts of Writing

METACONCEPT
Writing Is an Activity and a Subject of Study

Elizabeth Wardle and Linda Adler-Kassner

Writing is created, produced, distributed, and used for a variety of purposes. In this sense, it is an *activity* in which individuals and groups engage. However, the production, consumption, circulation, distribution, and use of writing are also areas of inquiry. Researchers in a number of fields (including, but not limited to, rhetoric and composition, linguistics, and literacy studies) investigate questions about writing. These include:

- How have forms of writing developed over time?
- What conceptions of writing do people have, and what values are suggested by these conceptions? What writing practices and processes are encouraged by these conceptions? Where do these conceptions come from?
- How is writing produced by individuals and groups, for what purposes, and with what implications or consequences?
- How are attitudes toward the production and uses of writing shaped by individuals and groups within specific contexts?
- How have different approaches to shaping the production of writing taken form, with what motivations, and to what ends?
- How is writing a technology, and how do writing technologies impact how writing happens and what can be done with writing?

Outside of scholars involved in the study of writing, the idea that writing is not only an activity in which people engage but also a subject of study often comes as a surprise, partially because people tend to experience writing as a finished product that represents ideas in seemingly rigid forms but also because writing is often seen as a "basic skill" that a person can learn once and for all and not think about again.

Research in writing and rhetoric has demonstrated that these ideas about writing do not match the ways that writing actually works and happens, but this more complex view of writing is not one that is widely shared or understood beyond the field. In fact, to be considered "successful," all writers must learn to study expectations for writing within specific contexts and participate in those to some degree.

The threshold concept that writing is a subject of study *as well as* an activity is troublesome because it contravenes popular conceptions of writing as a basic, ideology-free skill. When teachers and learners recognize writing as complex enough to require study, and recognize that the study of writing suggests they should approach, learn, and teach writing differently, they are then invited to behave differently and to change their conceptions of what writing is and their practices around writing that extend from those conceptions.

CONCEPT 1
Writing Is a Social and Rhetorical Activity

1.0

WRITING IS A SOCIAL AND RHETORICAL ACTIVITY
Kevin Roozen

It is common for us to talk about writing in terms of the particular text we are working on. Consider, for example, how often writers describe what they are doing by saying "I am writing an email" or "I'm writing a report" or "I'm writing a note." These shorthand descriptions tend to collapse the activity of writing into the act of single writer inscribing a text. In doing so, they obscure two foundational and closely related notions of writing: writers are engaged in the work of making meaning for particular audiences and purposes, and writers are always connected to other people.

Writers are always doing the rhetorical work of addressing the needs and interests of a particular audience, even if unconsciously. The technical writers at a pharmaceutical company work to provide consumers of medications with information they need about dosages and potential side effects. The father writing a few comments on a birthday card to his daughter crafts statements intended to communicate his love for her. Sometimes, the audience for an act of writing might be the writer himself. A young man jotting in his diary, for example, might be documenting life events in order to better understand his feelings about them. A child scribbling a phrase on the palm of her hand might do so as a way of reminding herself to feed the family pets, clean her room, or finish her homework. Writing, then, is always an attempt to address the needs of an audience.

In working to accomplish their purposes and address an audience's needs, writers draw upon many other people. No matter how isolated a writer may seem as she sits at her computer, types on the touchpad of her smartphone, or makes notes on a legal pad, she is always drawing upon the ideas and experiences of countless others. The technical writers at a pharmaceutical company draw collaboratively upon the ideas of others

DOI: 10.7330/9781607325789.c001

they work with as they read their colleagues' earlier versions of the information that will appear on the label. They also connect themselves to others as they engage with the laws about their products written by legislatures and the decisions of lawsuits associated with medications that have been settled or may be pending. The father crafting birthday wishes to his daughter might recall and consciously or unconsciously restate comments that his own parents included on the birthday cards he received as a child. As I work to craft this explanation of writing as a social and rhetorical activity, I am implicitly and explicitly responding to and being influenced by the many people involved in this project, those with whom I have shared earlier drafts, and even those whose scholarship I have read over the past thirteen years.

Writing puts the writer in contact with other people, but the social nature of writing goes beyond the people writers draw upon and think about. It also encompasses the countless people who have shaped the genres, tools, artifacts, technologies, and places writers act with as they address the needs of their audiences. The genres of medication labels, birthday wishes, and diary entries writers use have undergone countless changes as they have been shaped by writers in various times and places. The technologies with which writers act—including computer hardware and software; the QWERTY keyboard; ballpoint pens and lead pencils; and legal pads, journals, and Post-It notes—have also been shaped by many people across time and place. All of these available means of persuasion we take up when we write have been shaped by and through the use of many others who have left their traces on and inform our uses of those tools, even if we are not aware of it.

Because it conflicts with the shorthand descriptions we use to talk and think about writing, understanding writing as a social and rhetorical activity can be troublesome in its complexity. We say "I am writing an email" or "I am writing a note," suggesting that we are composing alone and with complete autonomy, when, in fact, writing can never be anything but a social and rhetorical act, connecting us to other people across time and space in an attempt to respond adequately to the needs of an audience.

While this concept may be troublesome, understanding it has a variety of benefits. If teachers can help students consider their potential audiences and purposes, they can better help them understand what makes a text effective or not, what it accomplishes, and what it falls short of accomplishing. Considering writing as rhetorical helps learners understand the needs of an audience, what the audience knows and does not know, why audience members might need certain kinds of information, what the audience finds persuasive (or not), and so on. Understanding the rhetorical work of writing is essential if writers are to make informed, productive decisions about which genres to employ, which languages to act with, which texts to reference, and so on. Recognizing the deeply social and rhetorical dimensions of writing can help administrators and other stakeholders make better decisions about curricula and assessment.

1.1

WRITING IS A KNOWLEDGE-MAKING ACTIVITY
Heidi Estrem

Writing is often defined by what it *is*: a text, a product; less visible is what it can *do*: generate new thinking (see 1.5, "Writing Mediates Activity"). As an activity undertaken to bring new understandings, writing in this sense is not about crafting a sentence or perfecting a text but about mulling over a problem, thinking with others, and exploring new ideas or bringing disparate ideas together (see "Metaconcept: Writing Is an Activity and a Subject of Study"). Writers of all kinds—from self-identified writers to bloggers to workplace teams to academic researchers—have had the experience of coming upon new ideas as a result of writing. Individually or in a richly interactive environment, in the classroom or workplace or at home, writers use writing to generate knowledge that they didn't have before.

Common cultural conceptions of the act of writing often emphasize magic and discovery, as though ideas are buried and the writer uncovers them, rather than recognizing that "the act of *creating* ideas, not finding them, is at the heart of significant writing" (Flower and Hayes 1980, 22; see also 1.9, "Writing Is a Technology through Which Writers Create and Recreate Meaning"). Understanding and identifying how writing is in itself an act of thinking can help people more intentionally recognize and engage with writing as a creative activity, inextricably linked to thought. We don't simply think first and then write (see 1.6, "Writing Is Not Natural"). We write *to* think.

Texts where this kind of knowledge making takes place can be formal or informal, and they are sometimes ephemeral: journals (digital and otherwise), collaborative whiteboard diagrams, and complex doodles and marginalia, for example. These texts are generative and central to meaning making even though we often don't identify them as such. Recognizing these kinds of texts for their productive value then broadens our understanding of literacy to include a rich range of everyday and workplace-based genres far beyond more traditionally recognized ones. Naming these as writing usefully makes visible the roles and purposes of writing (e.g., Barton and Hamilton 1998; Heath 2012).

Understanding the knowledge-making potential of writing can help people engage more purposefully with writing for varying purposes. In higher education, for example, faculty from across the curriculum now often include a wider range of writing strategies in their courses. That is, beyond teaching the more visible disciplinary conventions of writing in their fields, faculty also integrate writing assignments that highlight what is less visible but highly generative about writing in many contexts: writing's capacity for deeper understandings and new insights (see Anson 2010 for one historical account of the shift in how faculty from across campus teach writing). Beyond the classroom, people can employ exploratory, inquiry-based writing tasks like freewriting, planning, and mapping—sometimes individual and often collaborative. These strategies can help all writers increase their comprehension of subject material while also practicing with textual conventions in new genres. Through making the knowledge-making role of writing more visible, people gain experience with understanding how these sometimes-ephemeral and often-informal aspects of writing are critical to their development and growth.

1.2

WRITING ADDRESSES, INVOKES, AND/OR CREATES AUDIENCES
Andrea A. Lunsford

Writing is both relational and responsive, always in some way part of an ongoing conversation with others. This characteristic of writing is captured in what is referred to as the classic *rhetorical triangle*, which has at each of its points a key element in the creation and interpretation of meaning: writer (speaker, rhetor), audience (receiver, listener, reader), and text (message), all dynamically related in a particular context. Walter Ong (1975) referred to this history in his 1975 "The Writer's Audience is Always a Fiction," connecting the audience in oral performances with readers of written performances and exploring the ways in which the two differ. For Ong, the audience for a speech is immediately present, right in front of the speaker, while readers are absent, removed. Thus the need, he argues, for writers to fictionalize their audiences and, in turn, for audiences to fictionalize themselves—that is, to adopt the role set out for them by the writer.

Scholars in rhetoric and writing studies have extended this understanding of audience, explaining how writers can address audiences—that is, actual, intended readers or listeners—and invoke, or call up, imagined audiences as well. As I am writing this brief piece, for example, I am imagining or invoking an audience of students and teachers even as I am addressing the actual first readers of my writing, which in this case are the editors of this volume.

The digital age has brought with it the need for even closer consideration of audiences. We can no longer assume, for example, that the audience members for an oral presentation are actually present. And, especially in a digital age, writing cannot only address and invoke but also create audiences: as a baseball announcer in the film *Field of Dreams* (based on W. P. Kinsella's *Shoeless Joe*) says, "If you build it, they will come." Writers whose works have "gone viral" on the web know well what it means to create an audience that has been unintended and indeed unimagined. Perhaps even more important, the advent of digital and online literacies has blurred the boundaries between writer and audience significantly: the points of the once-stable rhetorical triangle seem to be twirling and shifting and shading into one another. When consumers of information can, quite suddenly, become producers as well, then it's hard to tell who is the writer, who the audience. In addition, the deeply collaborative and social nature of literacy in a digital age not only calls into question earlier distinctions but allows for greater agency on the part of both writers and audiences.

Such shifting and expanding understandings of audience and of the ways writers interact with, address, invoke, become, and create audiences raise new and important questions about the ethics of various communicative acts and call for pedagogies that engage students in exploring their own roles as ethical and effective readers/audiences/writers/speakers/listeners in the twenty-first century.

1.3

WRITING EXPRESSES AND SHARES MEANING TO BE RECONSTRUCTED BY THE READER

Charles Bazerman

The concept that writing expresses and shares meaning is fundamental to participating in writing—by writing we can articulate and communicate a thought, desire, emotion, observation, directive, or state of affairs to ourselves and others through the medium of written words.

The potential of making and sharing meaning provides both the motive and guiding principle of our work in writing and helps us shape the content of our communications. Awareness of this potential starts early in emergent literacy experiences and continues throughout one's writing life but takes on different force and depth as one continues through life.

The expression of meanings in writing makes them more visible to the writer, making the writer's thoughts clearer and shareable with others, who can attempt to make sense of the words, constructing a meaning they attribute to the writer. While writers can confirm that the written words feel consistent with their state of mind, readers can never read the writer's mind to confirm they fully share that state of mind. Readers share only the words to which each separately attributes meanings. Thus, meanings do not reside fully in the words of the text nor in the unarticulated minds but only in the dynamic relation of writer, reader, and text.

While a writer's meanings arise out of the expression of internal thought, the meanings attributed by a reader arise from the objects, experiences, and words available to that reader. For readers, the words of the text index or point to accessible ideas, thoughts, and experiences through which they can reconstruct meanings based on what they already know (see 3.3, "Writing Is Informed by Prior Experience").

Although meaning is philosophically complex, children readily grasp it in practice as they learn that they can share their experiences through writing about it. As their writing develops, they can express or articulate meanings more fully and precisely concerning a wider range of experiences, with wider audiences and with greater consequences.

The idea that writing expresses and shares meaning to be reconstructed by the reader can be troublesome because there is a tension between the expression of meaning and the sharing of it. Often, we view our expressions as deeply personal, arising from inmost impulses. We may not be sure others will respond well to our thoughts or will evaluate us and our words favorably. Therefore, every expression shared contains risk and can evoke anxiety. Writers often hesitate to share what they have expressed and may even keep private texts they consider most meaningful. Further, writers may resist the idea that their texts convey to readers something different than what the writers intended. Feedback from readers indicating that the writer's words do not convey all the writer hoped is not always welcomed (see 4.1, "Text Is an Object Outside of One's Self that Can Be Improved and Developed"; 5.2, "Metacognition Is Not Cognition"; and 4.4, "Revision Is Central to Developing Writing").

Awareness that meaning is not transparently available in written words may have the paradoxical effect of increasing our commitment to words as we mature as users of written language. As writers we may work on the words with greater care and awareness of the needs of readers so as to share our expressions of meaning as best as we can with the limited resources of written language. As readers we may increase our attention to reconstructing writers' meanings despite the fragility of words. The vagaries of meaning also may become a resource for us as writers, whether we are poets evoking readers' projections of personal associations or lawyers creating loopholes and compromises.

1.4

WORDS GET THEIR MEANINGS FROM OTHER WORDS

Dylan B. Dryer

This threshold concept is best illustrated with an example of how a particular word is defined and understood. If asked on the spot to define the word *cup*, an English speaker might say, "Well, it's a smallish drinking vessel, something you'd use for hot drinks like coffee or tea, so probably ceramic rather than glass; usually it has a little handle so your hand doesn't too hot." This is a perfectly serviceable definition, but the way it has been phrased glosses right over this threshold concept. To say that "a cup is a small ceramic drinking vessel" cannot be literally true, after all; the object used to serve hot drinks is not called into being by this sound, nor is there any reason for the phonemes symbolized by the three characters *c*, *u* and *p* to refer to this object (or to refer to it in English, at any rate; in German that object is referred to as *die Tasse*; in Mandarin as *Cháwǎn*; and so on.) Even English speakers don't always use that sound to mean a smallish ceramic drinking vessel. In the kitchen, *cup* is probably a unit of measure; in certain sporting circles, *cup* is the diminutive for the championship trophy (e.g., the Stanley Cup). *Cup* can even mean to hold something gingerly by not closing one's fingers about it, as one would cup an eggshell.

Cup does not have an especially elaborate range of meanings (consider words like *go* or *work* or *right*), but it adequately illustrates Ferdinand de Saussure's great insight: "In language itself, there are only differences" (Saussure 1983, 118). Saussure meant that because there is no necessary connection between any sounds or clusters of symbols and their referents (otherwise different languages would not exist), the meanings of words are relational—they acquire their meanings from other words. Any definition relies on words to explain what other words mean; moreover, words in a sentence or paragraph influence and often determine each other's meaning (which is why children are often advised to puzzle out an unfamiliar vocabulary word from its context). Slang terms for *good* and *bad* are particularly vivid examples of the ways context drives meaning—although these terms change practically overnight, their meanings are usually obvious because of the context of enthusiasm or disparagement in which they're uttered.

While the realization that words cannot be permanently linked to specific meanings can be disconcerting, the effects of this threshold concept are familiar. Most of us, for example, have had the unpleasant feeling that someone else has twisted our words or taken them out of context; we might have bristled at an excessively technical loophole someone finds in a seemingly sensible and obvious rule; we might have been startled by an interpretation of a familiar poem or a text we hold sacred (Meyer and Land 2006, 5). These experiences are reminders that the relations that imbue a sentence with particular meanings come not just from nearby words but also from the social contexts in which the sentence is used. For example, not only does each word in the four-word question "Ready for the cup?" combine with the other three to make the utterance understandable, but social context makes this question mean one thing in a kitchen and another thing while changing the channel at a sports bar. "Language," says Mikhail Bakhtin, "lies on the borderline between oneself and the other. The word in language is half someone else's" (Bakhtin 1981, 293).

This phenomenon works the other way, too: if meanings of words shift in response to changes in social contexts, it's also possible to infer changes in social contexts from changes in the meanings of words. In everyday usage, *text* is now almost exclusively a verb as the ubiquity of cell phones has changed our communication practices; changes in our thinking about gender representation have virtually eliminated the word *mankind* from public discourse; *green* has acquired a complex set of meanings in political, economic, and engineering contexts, and so on. And writers often give semantic drift deliberate shoves of their own, either by working to change what a word is perceived to mean (for example, "queer") or by placing familiar words in new contexts to provoke a new perspective; for example, Gloria Anzaldúa and Linda Brodkey have likened writing to "compustura" (Lunsford 1998, 9) and "stitching" (1994, 545–7), respectively—seaming together something different from existing material.

There are three important implications of understanding this threshold concept. First, when writers understand that meanings are not determined by history or *Webster's* prescriptions alone, but also by language users' contexts and motives, they gain a powerful insight into the causes of communicative success and failure. When readers and writers share a workplace, a close relationship, a broad set of assumptions, or the same field of study, they can rely on these social contexts to fill in the blanks with shared understanding (specialists conversing in technical jargon or lovers speaking in their private language, for example). But when readers and writers don't share close, intense contexts like these, they can have surprising reactions to even seemingly self-evident words like *justice, research, freedom, essay*, or *evidence*. To work with another simple example, Saussure used a drawing to represent the concept of tree evoked by the Latin word *arbor* and the equally arbitrary English *tree*. Suppose then that we surround the word *tree* with two different clusters of words, some drawn from communities reliant on the timber industry (*living wage, local economy, tradition*, and *skill*) and others drawn from communities reliant on tourism (*nature, habitat, preservation*, and *recreation*). It's not at all far from the truth to say we are speaking of two different trees. Even if we can agree in very broad particulars what *justice* means, our personal sense of what it means, the contexts in which we might use it, and the examples we might use to illustrate it will seldom map precisely onto readers' equally complex private sets of connotations for this word.

Second, since we must often communicate with those outside of our close social contexts, this threshold concept also helps us see how we can reduce the likelihood of misunderstandings. Certainly students are often exhorted to define their terms, but this concept helps explain why particular meanings for key terms in their writing can require careful framing. Part of this understanding involves a sense of when readers might need their expectations for certain words managed and/or redirected. These moves will not guarantee perfect understanding, but they can help increase the chances that readers will produce the particular meaning the writer intended. Instructors, too, should remember that common assignment verbs like *analyze, interpret, explain*, and *respond* have discipline-specific contexts.

Finally, and most excitingly, writers who understand that the definitions of any word develop from its usage realize that they, too, are part of this process; every instance of their language use works to preserve certain meanings and to advance others.

1.5

WRITING MEDIATES ACTIVITY
David R. Russell

Writing is a technology, a tool (see 1.9, "Writing Is a Technology through Which Writers Create and Recreate Meaning"). It is, in a material sense, nothing more than making marks on surfaces, whether of paper, stone, liquid-crystal screens, or a child's hand (the girl reminding herself to feed her dog we met in 1.0, "Writing Is a Social and Rhetorical Activity"). The marks may represent the sounds of speech (as in alphabetic scripts like English) or ideas (as in ideographic scripts like Chinese) or pictures (as in pictographic scripts like Cuneiform). But as we've seen in 1.1 and 1.3 ("Writing Is a Knowledge-Making Activity" and "Writing Expresses and Shares Meaning to be Reconstructed by the Reader"), the marks do not "contain" ideas or emotions or even meaning. People make something of them. They must read them and interpret them to act on them or think with them.

This physical presence of writing mediates—comes between, intervenes in—the activity of people (Russell 1995; Russell 1997). The white marks *S T O P* on a red hexagonal surface mediate the activity of the drivers who arrive at the intersection at about the same time. (Those written marks also help mediate the activity of a scofflaw driver with the police and the courts.)

Writing occupies an intermediate or middle position to form a connecting link that people use to coordinate their activity. Sometimes this is obvious, like the stop sign or laws or the constitution of a club or a nation. Sometimes writing mediates activity that is conflictual, like court proceedings—or even massively violent, like wars fought over interpretations of holy scripture. Sometimes it mediates the deepest human bonds (like the father writing a birthday card in 1.0, "Writing Is a Social and Rhetorical Activity").

Although other forms of communication (like speaking) also mediate activity, writing has several advantages (and disadvantages) over those forms. Depending on the surface and the writing instrument used, writing lasts longer than speech (unless a recording device "writes" the sound waves). More importantly, the marks can be copied and distributed over great distances, unlike (unrecorded) speech and most other symbols. Thus, writing can coordinate the activity of far more people over much longer periods of time. For example, the Ten Commandments, first written on stone, have shaped human activity for some three thousand years now.

People can also return to writing over and over, revise it and shape it relatively easily (though more easily with a word processor than a quill pen or chisel!). In this way writing is very useful for mediation of cognitive processes—thinking. Writing can mediate the *internal* activity of thought and emotion as well as *external* behavior. Internal thoughts and feelings can be externalized relatively quickly in writing, manipulated and revised rather easily (individually or with other people), then reinternalized, or stored for later comparison. People can compare earlier states of mind to later states and act accordingly (like the young man with his journal in 1.0, or scientists in a lab examining successive printouts from an instrument). In this way, the mediation of writing has been central to the development of knowledge, in science and the arts, and to education, as people write to learn as well as learn to write.

The concept that writing mediates human activity is troublesome because it goes against the usual concepts of writing as "just" transcribing ("writing down" or "writing up") thought or speech (see 1.6, "Writing Is Not Natural"). But it is a concept people unconsciously use every time they choose a medium of communication because of its properties (a text rather than a phone call, for example)—or forget those properties (when an affair is discovered by means of work emails that the lovers thought were "just" their intimate conversation). More importantly, it is a concept that lies behind the durable, and seemingly permanent, structures of our modern human institutions, whose ongoing activity would be impossible without the medium of writing. The institutions that form our modern lives—government, commerce, industry, the arts, sciences, and so on—are mediated by written marks in databases, laws, regulations, books, the Internet.

1.6

WRITING IS NOT NATURAL

Dylan B. Dryer

English speakers routinely talk about writing as if it were speech, characterizing their inability to understand a text as difficulty understanding what that text is "saying," speaking of a writer's "voice" or "tone," describing readers as an "audience," and so forth. This habit conceals an essential difference: speech is natural in the sense that as modern homo sapiens, we've been speaking to one another for nearly two hundred thousand years. Our speech has been bound up in complex feedback loops with our physiology (evidence suggests that our larynxes adapted during these millennia, gradually acquiring an extraordinary expressive range) and our cognition (note how quickly and easily almost all children acquire expressive fluency in their native language[s] and how eagerly and seemingly involuntarily most adults participate in children's efforts at language acquisition). It is at this point exceptionally difficult to tease human socialization and language apart (see Burke 1966). But it's essential to remember that while many older children and adults also routinely write, they do so by combining arrays of symbols *for* those sounds.

These symbols can do many things, as this collection illustrates, but they cannot "record" speech or thought in their original forms; they *translate* speech and thought into inscriptions. Others (if they know the code) must then try to reactivate these symbols into meaning. Writing is not even inevitable: after all, not all languages have writing, and no particular system of inscribing symbols (alphanumeric, ideographic, syllabic, abjadic, etc.) is an obvious complement to any particular family of languages. And even more to the point, we haven't been doing it all that long: as far as anyone can tell, inscriptive systems didn't start cropping up here and there until about 3000 BCE, and only a few members of those cultures would have used those systems. The century or so in which some cultures have attempted to teach inscriptive systems at a nearly universal scale is definitely not long enough to be able to identify specific selective effects this technology has had on our cognitive architecture or overall physiology.

Words like *inscriptions, symbols, code,* and *arrays* are intended to emphasize the *technological* dimension of writing, first systematically explored by Walter Ong over thirty years ago. While we usually reserve the word *technology* for recent innovations, any cultural artifact that mediates activity is a technology, including those that have become invisible through long use: roofs, coats, hammers, electric lighting, cooking pots, and so forth. While some typists no longer need to peek at their QWERTY keyboards, and most children gradually stop "drawing" letters and start "writing" them as the symbols for certain sounds become interiorized, these writers have naturalized their relationship with technological arrays, not taken the next logical or organic step in language acquisition and practice. Keyboards and other tools of inscription—pens, pencils, chalk, dry-erase markers, software for computers and cellphones—fade from consciousness through use, and it becomes hard to remember that even a stick used to scratch *L-O-V-E* in the sand is using a technology of conventionalized symbols for sounds. However, neither writing produced with technologies—all writing, in other words—nor written language itself can be said to be "natural" in the way that speech is.

While counterintuitive, denaturalizing writing is not difficult: the startling experience of attempting to sign a document with one's nondominant hand, for example, can be a disconcerting reminder of the time before muscle memory and cognitive routine habituated us to certain symbol shapes. Pairing a familiar translation with its original-language version or an hour spent learning to read short texts in a simple code like Wingdings font can expose the arbitrariness of symbol-phoneme relationships. But why do this at all, especially since habituated fluency with these symbols and their technologies of inscription are generally considered important indexes of our maturity as writers?

It's useful to remember that writing is not natural because writers tend to judge their writing processes too harshly—comparing them to the ease with which they usually speak. Speech, however, employs an extensive array of modalities unavailable to writing: gesture, expression, pacing, register, silences, and clarifications—all of which are instantaneously responsive to listeners' verbal and nonverbal feedback. Once it is understood that writing *itself* is a technology, comparisons to speech become obviously limited or downright misleading since no inscriptive system could possibly capture a language's full range of communicative potential.

Writers can also benefit from the realization that they needn't blame themselves for the shortcomings of the system they've inherited. The limitations of this system—confounding illogicalities in pronunciation and spelling (*choose* but *loose*; *wood* and *would*; *clout* but *doubt*); exasperating inconsistencies in what constitutes an "error" and for whom; the persistent gulf between writers' intentions and readers' interpretations—are simply inherent to a piecemeal technology encumbered with centuries of patchwork solutions to antiquated designs. This is not to say that these limitations are unimportant or ignorable. It is to say, however, that all writers are negotiating workarounds to the limitations of a technology they have inherited rather than bungling an obvious complement to the speech in which they have been naturally adept since childhood.

1.7

ASSESSING WRITING SHAPES CONTEXTS AND INSTRUCTION
Tony Scott and Asao B. Inoue

In school settings, writing assessment refers to the formulation of a judgment or decision based on the reading of student writing with a particular set of expectations or values in mind. Assessment thus encompasses a range of activities, from responding with revision in mind to evaluation or grading of final products to large-scale programmatic assessments.

Writing assessments are a social activity and can be shaped by a variety of individual or institutional factors, including stated goals for writing education; disciplinary philosophies of literacy and learning; political agendas; efficiency imperatives; or common cultural assumptions about writers and literacy. Because the judgments reflected in assessments are informed by factors like these, assessment is not neutral: it shapes the social and rhetorical contexts where writing takes place, especially in school. Any assessment or evaluation applies specific values and also encourages writers to adopt those values. How teachers or others assess student writing, what products those assessment processes produce (e.g., grades, comments on papers, decisions about students, responses to peers' drafts, etc.), and the consequences of those products all can *create* the very competencies any writing assessment says it measures (Gould 1981; Hanson 1993).

In other words, whatever is emphasized in an assessment produces what is defined as "good writing" in a class, a program, or a curriculum. Likewise, what is not emphasized becomes less important and may not be considered characteristic of good writing. For example, a classroom activity that asks students to identify and comment on the critical thinking occurring in peers' drafts emphasizes critical thinking as a part of what is good writing. By asking students to look for and evaluate critical thinking in drafts, teachers signal that they value critical thinking and encourage students to value it, possibly more than other elements one might find in drafts.

Writing assessment constructs boundaries for learning and student agency in learning environments and frames how students understand writing and their own abilities. It can therefore affect curricula, students' senses of their legitimacy and chances of success, and a teacher's job status, intellectual and creative agency, and merit.

Finally, assessment shapes relationships and power between teachers, students, and institutions. Depending on the institutional setting, teachers and students have varying degrees of agency to determine the character of their work, and teachers and students negotiate their relative authority, in part, through the ways students' writing is evaluated and the consequences associated with those evaluations. Institutions can use assessments to inform teachers and students while lending them agency, or they can align prescribed curricula with assessment outcomes to determine the focus of teaching and circumscribe the scope of students' writing. Writing assessment can thereby function as an intentional means of controlling the labor and creative latitude of teachers and students.

The assessment of writing shapes contexts and learning environments: it is a set of practices enacted by people in specific circumstances for specific purposes that have consequences for both the people whose writing is being judged and for those who are judging.

1.8

WRITING INVOLVES MAKING ETHICAL CHOICES

John Duffy

We tend to think of writing as an activity that involves communicating information, or making an argument, or expressing a creative impulse, even when we imagine it as something that creates meaning between writers and readers (see 1.2, "Writing Addresses, Invokes, and/ or Creates Audiences"). Writing is indeed all those things. But writing is equally an activity that involves ethical choices that arise from the relationship of writer and reader.

Writing involves ethical choices because every time we write for another person, we propose a relationship with other human beings, our readers. And in proposing such relationships we inevitably address, either explicitly and deliberately, or implicitly and unintentionally, the questions that moral philosophers regard as ethical: What kind of person do I want to be? How should I treat others? How should I live my life? (Shafer-Landau 2007). For writers, these questions may be rephrased: What kind of writer do I wish to be? What are my obligations to my readers? What effects will my words have upon others, upon my community?

To say that writing involves ethical choices is not to suggest that individual writers should be judged as ethical or unethical in the sense of being moral, upright, honest, and so forth. Nor it is to say that writers necessarily reflect on ethical concerns as they write. They may or may not. Neither is it to assert, finally, that every text can be regarded as ethical or unethical based on its content. Many texts, perhaps most, are devoid of the subject matter typically associated with ethics.

Rather, to say writing involves ethical choices is to say that when creating a text, the writer addresses others. And that, in turn, initiates a relationship between writer and readers, one that necessarily involves human values and virtues. A writer attempting to communicate an idea or persuade an audience, for example, may write in ways that privilege honesty, accuracy, fairness, and accountability. These qualities imply an attitude toward the writer's readers: in this case, attitudes of respect-fulness, open-mindedness, goodwill, perhaps humility. Conversely, an informational or persuasive text that is unclear, inaccurate, or deliber-ately deceptive suggests a different attitude toward readers: one that is at best careless, at worst contemptuous. (A close examination of what are commonly referred to as *logical fallacies* will show that these are better understood as ethical dispositions rather than as lapses of logic.) Writers of fiction or poetry, to take a different kind of example, may write in ways that privilege other virtues, such as playfulness, opacity, or original-ity. These, too, speak to the writer's conception of the reader and there-fore to the ethical considerations that follow when entering a relation-ship with another human being.

The understanding of writing as an act of ethical decision making unsettles conceptions of writing as solely instrumental, polemical, or aes-thetic. Beyond these, writing is also and perhaps ultimately understood as an activity that engages us with others and thus with problems asso-ciated with the moral life: What shall I say? To whom do I speak? What obligations follow from my words? What are the consequences? Whether or not the writer voices such questions, they are inherent in the act of communicating with another (see 1.3, "Writing Expresses and Shares Meaning to be Reconstructed by the Reader").

When we see writing this way, as an activity involving ethical choices arising from the human relationship of writer and readers, we cross a threshold that both expands and complicates our understandings of what it means to write.

1.9

WRITING IS A TECHNOLOGY THROUGH WHICH WRITERS CREATE AND RECREATE MEANING

Collin Brooke and Jeffrey T. Grabill

I. A. Richards once observed, "A book is a machine to think with" (Richards 2001). While we may think about texts differently than we do our automobiles or kitchen appliances, there is something suggestive about Richards's comparison that is worth pursuing. Writing is a tech-nology, and thinking of it in this fashion can be productive for both stu-dents and teachers of writing.

Writing has always been a technology for thinking and communicat-ing. Early inscription technologies enabled the organization of social practices (like commerce), and innovations in the organization of writing itself, such as the emergence of the book, helped create new social relationships. Whether we are talking about sound waves, physical marks on a page, or pixels rendered on the screen of a computer, tablet, or phone, writing makes material some version of the thoughts and ideas of its composer (see 1.1, "Writing Is a Knowledge-Making Activity"). The audience for such writing must similarly devote material resources to understanding it, even if simply in the form of attention (see 1.2, "Writing Addresses, Invokes, and/or Creates Audiences"). Meaning doesn't just happen.

The tools we use to produce writing (pens, keyboards) and those media where writing takes place (pages, books, screens) are all a part of what we mean when we describe writing as a technology. Tools and media shape what we are able to write and the ideas we can express, and they condition the expectations of those who read our writing. We might describe these qualities as the affordances of particular technologies (and environments), those features that permit certain actions (while perhaps limiting others). Writing an essay on a computer, for example, affords certain actions, such as the quick erasure or manipulation of text from words to sentences to paragraphs. Media carry different affordances. We think little of seeing hashtags in a Twitter feed, for instance, but many of us would find it quite distracting to read a novel with such language practices. Likewise, the ability to click on a hashtag in a tweet (and to see all the posts tagged thusly) is not an affordance of the printed page.

With the emergence and diffusion of digital technologies, however, the impact of technology on the making of meaning has never been more visible, socially and culturally. The power of networks can perhaps be most easily understood in terms of connectivity: the ability to connect readers to writers, to turn anyone with a network connection into a publisher. Connectivity allows writers to access and participate more seamlessly and quickly with others and to distribute writing to large and widely dispersed audiences. Many writing technologies have streamlined the writing process, but the computer network has had a dramatic social impact. Consider, for example, platforms like Facebook and *Wikipedia*, arguably two of the most significant collaborative writing projects in human history. The affordances of particular writing technologies participate in the construction of new and changing rhetorical contexts.

Writers may prefer different tools and/or environments depending on their affordances, yet it has become more difficult to separate the scene of writing from the tools we use to produce it. This is because writing, as it always has been, is a technology for thinking, and so it may be the case that we interiorize the technology of writing itself to shape the possibilities for meaning.

References

Anson, Chris. 2010. "The Intradisciplinary Influence of Composition and WAC, 1967–1986." *WAC Journal* 21: 5–19.

Bakhtin, M. M. 1981. "Discourse in the Novel." In *The Dialogic Imagination*, edited by Michael Holquist. Translated by Caryl Emerson and Michael Holquist., 259–422. Austin: University of Texas Press.

Barton, David, and Mary Hamilton. 1998. *Local Literacies: Reading and Writing in One Community*. London: Routledge. http://dx.doi.org/10.4324/9780203448885.

Brodkey, Linda. 1994. "Writing on the Bias." College English 56 (5): 527–47.

Burke, Kenneth. 1966. "Definition of Man." In *Language as Symbolic Action: Essays on Life, Literature, and Method*, ed. Kenneth Burke, 3–24. Berkeley: University of California Press.

Flower, Linda, and John Hayes. 1980. "The Cognition of Discovery: Defining a Rhetorical Problem." *College Composition and Communication* 31 (1): 21–32.

Gould, Stephen J. 1981. *The Mismeasure of Man*. New York: W. W. Norton.

Hanson, F. Allan. 1993. *Testing Testing: Social Consequences of the Examined Life*. Berkeley: University of California Press.

Heath, Shirley Brice. 2012. *Words at Work and Play: Three Decades in Family and Community Life*. Cambridge: Cambridge University Press.

Lunsford, Andrea A. 1998. "Toward a Mestiza Rhetoric: Gloria Anzaldúa on Composition and Postcoloniality." *JAC: A Journal of Composition Theory* 18 (1): 1– 27.

Meyer, Jan H. F., and Ray Land. 2006. "Threshold Concepts and Troublesome Knowledge: An Introduction." In *Overcoming Barriers to Student Understanding*, edited by Jan H. F. Meyer and Ray Land, 3–18. London: Routledge.

Ong, Walter. 1975. "The Writer's Audience is Always a Fiction." *PMLA* 90 (1): 9–21.

Richards, I. A. 2001. *Principles of Literary Criticism*. 2nd ed. London: Routledge.

Russell, David R. 1995. "Activity Theory and Its Implications for Writing Instruction." In *Reconceiving Writing, Rethinking Writing Instruction*, edited by Joseph Petraglia, 51–77. Mahwah, NJ: Erlbaum.

Russell, David R. 1997. "Rethinking Genre in School and Society: An Activity Theory Analysis." *Written Communication* 14 (4): 504–54. http://dx.doi.org/10.1177/0741088 397014004004.

Saussure, Ferdinand de. 1983. *Course in General Linguistics*. Translated by Roy Harris. Chicago: Open Court.

Shafer-Landau, Russ, ed. 2007. *Ethical Theory: An Anthology*. Malden: Blackwell.

CONCEPT 2
Writing Speaks to Situations through Recognizable Forms

2.0

WRITING SPEAKS TO SITUATIONS
THROUGH RECOGNIZABLE FORMS
Charles Bazerman

A fundamental problem in communication precedes the choosing of any words or shaping of any message: identifying the situation we are in and the nature of the communication we wish to make. Are salespeople offering us a deal and do we want to accept? Are our acquaintances amusing each other with jokes and are we amused? Are our trusted advisors asking us to reconsider our behaviors and do we resist? The situation frames our understanding of the communicative action of others and gives us the urgency and motive to respond because somehow we sense our words will satisfy our needs in the situation or otherwise make the situation better for us. In face-to-face life, this problem is solved through our recognizing the geographic locale we are in, the people we are talking to, our relationship to them, the events unfolding before us, and our impulses to do something. Through long practical experience we learn to recognize spontaneously what appears to be going on around us and how it affects us. Our impulses to act communicatively emerge as doable actions in the situation, in forms recognizable to others—we accept the offer, we laugh at the joke, we agree to change. Conscious thought is warranted only if we have reason to believe things are not as they appear to be, if confusions arise within the situation, or if we want to suppress our first impulse and pursue a less obvious strategic path—laughing to appear congenial though we find the joke offensive.

Writing, as well, addresses social situations and audiences organized in social groups and does so through recognizable forms associated with those situations and social groups. But with writing we have fewer here-and-now clues about what the situation is, who our audiences are, and how we want to respond. Written messages can circulate from one material and social situation to another, and in fact are usually intended to.

DOI: 10.7330/9781607325789.c002

A newspaper report about events in one city is read in another, even in another country, and further events have evolved between writing and reading. A poem written for a small circle of friends is read centuries later in a literature classroom.

The technical concept of rhetorical situation brings together recognition of the specifics of the situation, the exigency the situation creates, and our perception that by communication we can make the situation better for ourselves (Bitzer 1968). Awareness of rhetorical situation is the beginning of reflection on how we perceive the situation, what more we can understand about it, how we can formulate our goals, and what strategies we may take in our utterances. It helps us put in focus what we can accomplish in a situation, how we can accomplish it, and what the stakes are. But this awareness also puts a reflective distance between our perception of the situation and our responses, which may disrupt spontaneous impulses and our sense of being in the moment. This disruption can thus can be troublesome and require a fundamental reorientation toward our experiences, which we may at first resist. Recognizing we are being accused of misdeeds may make us aware we need to answer but also aware that we must frame our words carefully so as to defend ourselves persuasively and so as not to lead to further trouble or accusations.

With writing, the need for understanding the rhetorical situation is even greater than in speaking because there are fewer material clues with which to locate ourselves spontaneously. To engage in a disciplinary discussion in chemistry, we not only need to know the chemistry, we need to know how each text is entering into a debate or accumulating past findings or projecting future plans (see 2.3, "Writing Is a Way of Enacting Disciplinarity"). It is through genre that we recognize the kinds of messages a document may contain, the kind of situation it is part of and it might migrate to, the kinds of roles and relations of writers and readers, and the kinds of actions realized in the document (see 1.2, "Writing Addresses, Invokes, and/or Creates Audiences," and 2.2, "Genres Are Enacted by Writers and Readers"). Genre recognition provides a necessary clue for locating and making sense of any piece of paper or any digital display that comes before our eyes. Perhaps even more complexly, we may need to understand how documents move from among and between spaces, including from real spaces to enduring virtual spaces, which then may return to specific material spaces. So, teachers may collect records of students within a classroom for immediate classroom-management needs, but these records then may enter the school records for school-management purposes and then may be combined with school medical and other records to create a file on the student, creating an enduring characterization of the student that may reappear in a court proceeding. Thus, to understand the full range of situations a document in a particular genre may be used in and the full set of meanings that might be attributed to it, we also need to understand the activity system it is part of (Russell 1997) (see 1.0, "Writing Is a Social and Rhetorical Activity," and 1.5, "Writing Mediates Activity").

Yet while writing may require more awareness of genres, the associated situations, and the activity systems those genres are part of, several factors limit conscious, reflective examination of genres and an understanding of their implications for the variability of writing. First, much learning of writing is in school, where stylized and repetitive classroom relations and situations, teacher authority, and student display of competence prevail. People often take school-based assumptions with them long after they leave school, associating writing with particular kinds of school assignments and finding their main motives to be avoiding correction and getting a good grade.

Later, after schooling, if they become deeply embedded in a set of writing practices associated with their profession or career, they may then assume, with little conscious attention to how complex and varied situations, exigencies, motives, and genres may be, that what they learn in that specific context are general rules and models for effective writing—with the result that they overgeneralize the practices they have learned. Further, they may think of the writing practices they develop through long professional experience to be part of their profession and may think of how they produce their texts as a matter of just doing good science, or being a good salesman, or knowing how to keep good records of what happens. Their writing knowledge, knowledge of situations, and sense of genres becomes deeply tacit and less accessible to conscious reflection. However, bringing such things to reflective attention through the concepts of rhetorical situation, genre, and activity systems is a necessary step to understanding their writing and making deeper choices.

2.1

WRITING REPRESENTS THE WORLD, EVENTS, IDEAS, AND FEELINGS
Charles Bazerman

It is no surprise to people that they can talk or write about things they see or do, what they feel, and what they think. But it is something of a surprise to realize that how each of these is represented in the writing or speaking—in other words, in the communication—changes what is shared about each of them and thus what our common knowledge is. I may think if I write about a mountain that the mountain is there for all to see, so the words I use are not that important. But when I realize that all my readers are likely to know of the mountain, particularly on a sunny early spring afternoon after an overnight snow storm ending in sleet so the crust breaks through unpredictably beneath the feet, is through the words I write, I begin to take greater care in choosing my words. I want to represent facts, the world, or my imaginings as precisely and powerfully as I can. We may resist this idea because we think the world and the meaning of our ideas are more robust than the words we choose, or because grappling with words is hard and frustrating work, and we may feel that our words are always a reduction, always lose something. That is indeed so. But because words are such thin and frail communicators, writers must work hard to make them do the best they can do.

A further troublesome corollary is that what we can share with each other through writing is limited by our ability to represent the world through language and the ability of our readers to make sense of our representations in ways congruent to our intentions (see 1.2, "Writing Addresses, Invokes, and/or Creates Audiences," and 1.3, "Writing Expresses and Shares Meanings to Be Reconstructed by the Reader"). Writers often have great ambitions about the effects and power of what they write and their ability to capture the truth of realities or conjure imagined realities, but they are constantly caught up short by what they can bring into shared reality through words. Recognizing the limitations of our representations can lead us to appropriate modesty and caution about what we and others write and about decisions and calculations made on the basis of the representations. Alfred Korzybski stated this concept vividly by noting "the map is not the territory" (Korzybski 1958, 58). Yet knowledge of this concept helps us work more effectively from our verbal maps in the way we view and contemplate the world represented.

Despite the limits of language, most of what we consider knowledge comes from the representation of the world and events in texts (see 1.1, "Writing Is a Knowledge-Making Activity"). Will Rogers famously said, "All I know is what I read in the newspapers." The humor and humility in his statement are precisely in the recognition that most of our knowledge comes from the texts we read. If people don't share those texts (or other texts derivative of the primary representation), they don't share the knowledge. The recognition that different statements representing knowledge circulate in different groups does not mean all representations are equal, but it focuses our attention on the procedures and criteria by which these representations enter a communicative network and are evaluated, held accountable, and established as credible. People may resist this recognition as it destabilizes the absoluteness of knowledge and seems to undermine certainty of truth, but recognition of this concept provides a path to a more detailed understanding of how things reach the status of truth within different communities and the criteria by which truth is held. Knowing this can help us write more carefully and effectively to represent the world, events, and ideas credibly within and across communities and to discuss the representations of others in relation to the social worlds the knowledge circulates within.

2.2

GENRES ARE ENACTED BY WRITERS AND READERS
Bill Hart-Davidson

One of the more counterintuitive ideas in writing studies has to do with the nature of a genre—not just how the term is defined but also about what genres are. Common-sense notions of *genre* hold that that the term describes a form of discourse recognizable as a common set of structural or thematic qualities. People may speak about detective novels as a genre distinct from romance novels, for instance. We can also recognize nonliterary forms as genres, such as the scientific article.

In writing studies, though, the stabilization of formal elements by which we recognize genres is seen as the visible effects of human *action*, routinized to the point of habit in specific cultural conditions. The textual structures are akin to the fossil record left behind, evidence that writers have employed familiar discursive moves in accordance with reader expectations, institutional norms, market forces, and other social influences.

The idea that genres are enacted is associated most strongly, perhaps, with Carolyn Miller's argument in a 1984 article in the *Quarterly Journal of Speech* titled "Genres as Social Action." Miller's (1984) argument was influenced by Mikhail Bakhtin (1986), and has been developed over the last thirty years by a number of scholars studying writing in organizational settings such as David Russell (1991), Charles Bazerman (1988), and Catherine Schryer (1993), among many others.

This view holds that genres are habitual responses to recurring socially bounded situations. Regularities of textual form most lay people experience as the structural characteristics of genres emerge from these repeated instances of action and are reinforced by institutional power structures. Genres are constructions of groups, over time, usually with the implicit or explicit sanction of organizational or institutional power.

This view of genre has several interesting implications most newcomers to the idea find challenging and fascinating. One is that no single text is a genre; it can only be an instance of that genre as it enters into contexts (activity systems) where it might be taken up as such an instance. Readers and users of texts have as much to do with a text becoming an instance of a genre as writers do (see 1.2, "Writing Addresses, Invokes, and/or Creates Audiences,"). And because creating a genre is not something an individual writer does, but rather is the result of a series of socially mediated actions that accumulate over time, genres are only *relatively* stable. Generic forms are open to hybridization and change over time. This is why Schryer refers to the textual features of genres as "stable for now" forms, acknowledging that they can evolve.

JoAnneYates (1993) offers a fascinating historical account of this sort of genre hybridization in the context of the rise of American industrialization. In this account, we learn that standard features of genres, such as the header block of a business memo appearing in the upper left corner, become stable in use situations. When documents were stored in vertical stacks rather than in file cabinets, the memo block allowed for easy search and retrieval. This convention remains today even in email though we no longer need to flip through hard copies to find a message. As we might expect, the convention is less stable due to changes in the use context; users can choose to hide or minimize headers, for instance, in many email programs.

2.3

WRITING IS A WAY OF ENACTING DISCIPLINARITY
Neal Lerner

The central claim of this threshold concept is that disciplines shape—and in turn are shaped by—the writing that members of those disciplines do. In sum, the relationship between disciplinary knowledge making and the ways writing and other communicative practices create and communicate that knowledge are at the heart of what defines particular disciplines.

As an example of the relationship between writing and disciplinarity, consider the use of citations. On the most visible level, citation practices vary by discipline—and often within subdisciplines. Whether the practice is an author-last-name parenthetical system, author-last-name-plus-date parenthetical citation, footnotes, or numbered references, disciplinary distinctions are clearly marked, and readers in those disciplines have clear expectations for what type of citation formats they will encounter. Different formats also convey different disciplinary values. For example, formats that include the date in a parenthetical citation (e.g., APA) convey to readers that timeliness is important to that discipline; in contrast, formats that only include authors' last names (e.g., MLA) convey the value that references are timeless in certain ways.

Citation practices also enact disciplinarity on more subtle levels (see, e.g., Bazerman 1987; Connors 1999; Hyland 1999; Swales 1990). The mechanics used to introduce previously published work—for example, a parenthetical reference or footnote versus an attributive phrase—convey distinct disciplinary values. Citations tell us something about the discipline's values and practices while also recreating them by enacting them.

On a larger discourse level, any disciplinary genre speaks to the processes by which members of a discipline shape, make distinct, and value its forms and practices of knowledge creation and communication, and these processes, in turn, are shaped by the histories of those genres (see 2.0, "Writing Speaks to Situations through Recognizable Forms"). For example, the experimental report in science has evolved over several hundred years into the IMRD format—introduction, methods, results, discussion—an organizational scheme meant to mimic the scientific research process, particularly as that process has become more codified (Bazerman 1988). In contrast, while a short story also has specific features meant to function in specific ways for a specific disciplinary audience, readers would be hard pressed to confuse a short story with an experimental report. Many distinct disciplinary genres—e.g., legal briefs, SOAP notes, mathematical proofs—reflect the values those disciplines assign to particular kinds of evidence, particular forms of argument, and particular expectations for the transaction between readers and writers in particular rhetorical situations (see 2.0, "Writing Speaks to Situations through Recognizable Forms").

Of course, disciplinary boundaries can sometimes be quite fluid rather than fixed and stable. Such fluidity offers further evidence that disciplinary knowledge making is a social process and subject to changing norms, practices, and technologies (Thaiss and Zawacki 2006; also see 1.9 "Writing Is a Technology through Which Writers Create and Recreate Meaning"). Ultimately, writers and readers come to writing in their disciplines with histories, intentions, and expectations, all shaping the disciplines themselves and, in turn, shaping the writing that members of those disciplines do.

2.4

ALL WRITING IS MULTIMODAL
Cheryl E. Ball d Colin Charlton

Multimodal means "multiple + mode." In contemporary writing studies, a mode refers to a way of meaning making, or communicating. The New London Group (NLG) outlines five modes through which meaning is made: linguistic, aural, visual, gestural, and spatial. Any combination of modes makes a multimodal text, and all texts—every piece of communication a human composes—use more than one mode. Thus, all writing is multimodal (New London Group 1996).

Historically, rhetoric and composition studies is often assumed to focus on writing (and sometimes speech) as solely alphanumeric-based communication—what the NLG would label as part of the linguistic mode of communication. The term *mode*, within this historical perception, was reserved for defining the rhetorical modes of exposition, argumentation, description, and narration. In multimodal theory, the definition of *mode* is complicated to distribute equal emphasis on how meanings are created, delivered, and circulated through choices in design, material composition, tools and technologies, delivery systems, and interpretive senses (see 1.3, "Writing Expresses and Shares Meaning to Be Reconstructed by the Reader," and 1.9, "Writing Is a Technology through Which Writers Create and Recreate Meaning"). That is, *mode* isn't just words (in the linguistic sense of NLG's framework) but sound, texture, movement, and all other communicative acts that contribute to the making of meaning.

While the concept of multimodality has enjoyed increased circulation since the turn of the twenty-first century and has been associated with new media or new technologies, rhetoric and composition's historic approach to the teaching of writing has almost always included the production of multimodal texts. This understanding can be traced from classical rhetorical studies of effective speech design including body and hand gestures to current concerns with infographics and visual rhetorics.

With this context in mind, there are still two major misconceptions associated with multimodality. First, some assume all multimodal texts are digital. While it's true that most writing and design work in the twenty-first century is mediated through digital technologies such as computers, smartphones, or tablets, many texts that might be produced with digital technologies aren't necessarily distributed with digital technologies (e.g., posters, flyers, brochures, memos, some reports, receipts, magazines, books, scholarly print-based articles, etc.). In addition, many texts are not digital in their production *or* distribution ('zines, paintings, scrapbooks, etc.).

Second, some assume that the opposite of multimodal is monomodal. In fact, there is no such thing as a monomodal text. This assumption is a throwback to the romantic version of writing as focusing solely on alphanumeric textual production and analysis and is often used by scholar-teachers new to multimodal theory as a way to distinguish between "old" ways of researching and teaching writing and "new," multimodal ways (see the discussion of writing and disciplinarity in 2.3, "Writing Is a Way of Enacting Disciplinarity"). An example of a text often referred to as being monomodal is the traditional first-year-composition research essay (see 2.0, "Writing Speaks to Situations through Recognizable Forms"). Yet such a text is recognized from its linguistic mode and its visual and spatial arrangement on the page (title, name block, double spacing, margins, default font size, formulaic structure, etc.).

Monomodality, then, is used (incorrectly) to signify a lack of multiple media or modes when really what a user might mean is that a structure like a five-paragraph essay *privileges* the linguistic mode over the spatial or visual modes. Thus, writing as a knowledge-making activity (see 2.0, "Writing Speaks to Situations through Recognizable Forms") isn't limited to understanding writing as a single mode of communication but as a multimodal, performative (see 1.5, "Writing Mediates Activity," and 2.5, "Writing Is Performative") activity that takes place within any number of genres (see 2.2, "Genres Are Enacted by Writers and Readers") and disciplines.

2.5

WRITING IS PERFORMATIVE

Andrea A. Lunsford

Students are sometimes puzzled by the notion that writing is performative. Yet some discussion usually clarifies the concept as students quickly see that their writing performs for a grade or other reward for an audience of academics (mostly teachers; see 1.7, "Assessing Writing Shapes Contexts and Instruction"). In these pieces of writing, students might adopt a role or persona—of the "good student," for example. But writing is performative in other important senses as well. Kenneth Burke's concept of "language as symbolic action" helps explain why (Burke 1966). For Burke and other contemporary theorists, language and writing have the capacity to act, to do things in the world. Speech act theorists such as J. L. Austin (1962) speak of "performatives," by which they mean spoken phrases or sentences that constitute an action: a judge saying "I now pronounce you husband and wife" or "I sentence you to X" actually performs these acts. Other examples ("I bequeath" in a will or "I name this ship the Enterprise") carry such performativity (see 2.6, "Texts Get Their Meaning from Other Texts").

But we can see other ways in which writing performs: from the Declaration of Independence to the petition that results in a change of policy to a Kickstarter site whose statements are so compelling that they elicit spontaneous donations, writing has the capacity to perform. At its most basic, saying that writing is performative means that writing *acts*, that it can make things happen. This is what students in the Stanford Study of Writing, a longitudinal exploration of writing development during the college years, meant when they told researchers over and over again that "good writing is writing that makes something good happen in the world."

There is yet a third way in which writing can be said to be performative, and that is in relation to another threshold concept, that writing is *epistemic*. That is to say that writing does not simply record thought or knowledge but rather that writing has the capacity to actually produce thought and knowledge (see 3.0, "Writing Enacts and Creates Identities and Ideologies"). Most writers have experienced this performative aspect of writing—a time when you are writing away and the writing suddenly gives rise to new ideas, new insights into your topic. In the moment of producing such insights, writing is, again, performative.

2.6

TEXTS GET THEIR MEANING FROM OTHER TEXTS

Kevin Roozen

If I were to ask a writer or reader what the text in front of her means, it would be easy to assume that *text* refers only to the text immediately at hand. This assumption, though, overlooks the fact that whatever meaning a writer or reader makes of a particular text is not a result of their engagements with that particular text alone. Rather than existing as autonomous documents, texts always refer to other texts and rely heavily on those texts to make meaning. Although we commonly refer to *a* text or *the* text, texts are profoundly intertextual in that they draw meaning from a network of other texts. As a field, writing studies has developed a number of names for the networks of texts writers and readers create and act with, including *landscapes, sets, systems, ecologies, assemblages, repertoires,* and *intertexts.*

Some of the texts that contribute to the creation of meaning— for both writers and readers—are those that already exist. Thomas Jefferson's crafting of the Declaration of Independence, for example, was informed explicitly and implicitly by a vast network of previous texts that included Locke's writings on social contract theory, resolutions written by the First Continental Congress and other political bodies, political pamphlets, newspaper articles, a colonial play, the writings of Euripides, and the drafts and revisions offered by other members of Congress. Writers and readers rely on these kinds of intertextual linkages to make meaning of all kinds of texts. Children reading *Winnie the Pooh* for the first time might think about other books they have read or that have been read to them about forests, stuffed bears, or animals. Shoppers jotting grocery lists might rely on previous lists they have created and used or seen others use. Insurance processors adjusting claims might draw upon their previous encounters with the particular forms they need to read and fill out. Other texts drawn into an intertextual network are those the reader or writer might anticipate acting with in the future. A student taking notes while attempting to understand a philosophy text might also be thinking toward the essay exam at the end of the semester. A Supreme Court justice writing an opinion likely to be challenged in the future might craft it in a way that heads off particular legal arguments but leaves open others. The meaning writers and readers work to make of a given text at hand, then, is a function of the interplay of texts from their near and distant pasts as well as their anticipated futures.

Texts even rely upon a range of nonwritten texts. Readers and writers, for example, might draw upon visual images as they engage with a focal text. The child's reading of *Winnie the Pooh* might be informed by pictures or video images she has seen of the characters and scenes from the book. The shopper might use the images on coupons as a way to remember which items to include on next week's grocery list. Texts might also be linked to inscriptions such as charts, diagrams, and tables. Adjusting the insurance claim might involve the processor in looking up pricing data in a set of Excel charts, creating a digital drawing of an automobile accident, or interpreting schematics of automobile parts. Texts might also emerge from instances of talk. The philosophy student's notes, for example, might include comments offered by classmates during a class discussion or by a roommate. In drafting an opinion, the Supreme Court justice might draw upon conversations with clerks or with other justices.

The concept of texts getting their meaning from other texts may conflict with dominant Western notions of authorship, creativity, and originality, but it is an important one for a number of stakeholders. For teachers, recognizing that texts work in conjunction with other texts is a key first step toward creating opportunities for students to engage with a wide variety of texts, perhaps even ones that might not be privileged in formal educational settings. It is also a key step toward teachers acknowledging, valuing, and fostering connections with the different kinds of texts that animate learners' lives beyond the classroom. For learners, recognizing that texts get their meaning from other texts is the first step toward thinking carefully and creatively about how forging and reconfiguring linkages to other texts and even other contexts can shift meaning in ways both subtle and profound. This realization, in turn, can lead learners toward strategies for writing and reading that foreground the role of other texts. For administrators, conceptualizing the intertextual nature of writing and reading provides the foundation for thinking carefully and systematically about the kinds of texts learners need to encounter at particular points throughout the curriculum. For writing researchers, recognizing the intertextual nature of meaning making is the vital first step toward developing theoretical perspectives and methodological approaches for tracing the textual connections persons and collectives employ in the continual making and remaking of knowledge, selves, and societies.

References

Austin, J. L. 1962. *How to Do Things with Words.* Oxford: Clarendon Press.

Bakhtin, M. M. 1986. "The Problem of Speech Genres." In *Speech Genres and Other Late Essays,* edited by Caryl Emerson and Michael Holquist. Translated by Vernon W. McGee, 60–102. Austin: University of Texas Press.

Bazerman, Charles. 1987. "Codifying the Social Scientific Style: The APA Publication Manual as a Behaviorist Rhetoric." In *The Rhetoric of the Human Sciences,* edited by John Nelson, Allan Megill, and Donald McCloskey, 125–44. Madison: University of Wisconsin Press.

Bazerman, Charles. 1988. *Shaping Written Knowledge: The Genre and Activity of the Experimental Article in Science.* Madison: University of Wisconsin Press.

Bitzer, Lloyd F. 1968. "The Rhetorical Situation." *Philosophy & Rhetoric* 1 (1): 1–14.

Burke, Kenneth. 1966. *Language as Symbolic Action.* Berkeley: University of California Press.

Connors, Robert J. 1999. "The Rhetoric of Citation Systems: Part 2, Competing Epistemic Values in Citation." *Rhetoric Review* 17 (2): 219–45. http://dx.doi.org/10.1080/07350 199909359242.

Hyland, Ken. 1999. "Academic Attribution: Citation and the Construction of Disciplinary Knowledge." *Applied Linguistics* 20 (3): 341–67. http://dx.doi.org/10.1093/applin /20.3.341.

Korzybski, Alfred. 1958. *Science and Sanity: An Introduction to Non-Aristotelian Systems and General Semantics.* Brooklyn: Institute of General Semantics.

Miller, Carolyn. 1984. "Genre as Social Action." *Quarterly Journal of Speech* 70 (2): 151–67. http://dx.doi.org/10.1080/00335638409383686.

New London Group. 1996. "A Pedagogy of Multiliteracies: Designing Social Futures." *Harvard Educational Review* 66 (1). http://wwwstatic.kern.org/filer/blogWrite44Ma-nilaWebsite/paul/articles/A_Pedagogy_of_Multiliteracies_Designing_Social_Futures .htm.

Russell, David R. 1991. *Writing in the Academic Disciplines, 1870–1990: A Curricular History.* Carbondale: Southern Illinois University Press.

Russell, David R. 1997. "Rethinking Genre in School and Society: An Activity Theory Analysis." *Written Communication* 14 (4): 504–54. http://dx.doi.org/10.1177/0741088 397014004004.

Schryer, Catherine F. 1993. "Records as Genre." *Written Communication* 10 (2): 200–34. http://dx.doi.org/10.1177/0741088393010002003.

Swales, John. 1990. *Genre Analysis: English in Academic and Research Settings.* Cambridge: Cambridge University Press.

Thaiss, Chris, and Terri Zawacki. 2006. *Engaged Writers, Dynamic Disciplines.* Portsmouth: Heinemann, Boynton/Cook.

Yates, JoAnne. 1993. *Control through Communication: The Rise of System in American Management.* Vol. 6. Baltimore: Johns Hopkins University Press.

CONCEPT 3
Writing Enacts and Creates Identities and Ideologies

3.0

WRITING ENACTS AND CREATES IDENTITIES AND IDEOLOGIES
Tony Scott

An ideology is a system of ideas and beliefs that together constitute a comprehensive worldview. We make sense of the world around us *through* the ideologies to which we have been exposed and conditioned. Ideologies are both formed and sustained by a variety of factors, including religions, economic systems, cultural myths, languages, and systems of law and schooling. A common assumption in humanities theory and research is that there is no ideology-free observation or thought. Our conceptions of everything—gender identities and roles, people's proper social statuses, what it means to love, the proper basis for separating what is true from what is false—are inescapably shaped by ideologies. To be immersed in any culture is to learn to see the world through the ideological lenses it validates and makes available to us. Writing is always ideological because discourses and instances of language use do not exist independently from cultures and their ideologies.

Linguist James Paul Gee points out that those who seek to create any education program in reading and writing must ask a question: "What sort of social group do I intend to apprentice the learner into?" (Gee 2008, 48). This seemingly innocent question is actually quite loaded because it starts from the premise that there is no general literacy: literacy is always in some way involved in the negotiation of identities and ideologies in specific social situations. Vocabularies, genres, and language conventions are a part of what creates and distinguishes social groups, and thus learning to write is always ongoing, situational, and involving cultural and ideological immersion. This thinking represents a fundamental shift in how many writing scholars now see literacy education, from a view that is individualistic and focused on the acquisition of discrete, universal skills to one that is situated and focused on social involvement and consequences (see 1.0, "Writing Is a Social and

DOI: 10.7330/9781607325789.c003

Rhetorical Activity"). Writers are not separate from their writing and they don't just quickly and seamlessly adapt to new situations. Rather, writers are socialized, changed, through their writing in new environments, and these changes can have deep implications. For instance, when students learns to write convincingly as undergraduate college students in an introductory writing class, they enact that identity based on their reading of the expected and acceptable social norms. So in their writing, they might be inquisitive, deliberative, and given to founding their opinions on careful reasoning and research. In displaying these characteristics in their writing, they enact an identity in response to social expectations for who they are and what they should be doing.

This social view of ideology in writing studies has been influenced by the work of Lev Vygotsky (1978) and Mikhail Bakhtin (1986). Drawing on research on language acquisition in children, Vygotsky described how external speech becomes internalized and then comes to frame how we think, self-identify, and act in the world. As we are immersed in discourses through reading and dialogue with others, we begin to name and understand *through* those discourses, internalizing the ideologies they carry. Indeed, language learning and use is a primary means through which ideologies are conveyed, acquired, and made to seem "natural," without obvious alternatives or need of explanation. As ideological activity, writing is deeply involved in struggles over power, the formation of identities, and the negotiation, perpetuation, and contestation of belief systems. We can see obvious ideological tensions all around us in public political discourse: Do you use *climate change* or *global warming*? Does the United States have an issue with "illegals" or "undocumented immigrants"? Perhaps less obvious but highly consequential examples are embedded in everyday writing. In writing in professional contexts, for instance, writers can gain credibility and persuasive power through showing they understand and share the beliefs and values that are commonplace, and markers of fuller socialization, within their professions. When lawyers write effective briefs, or engineers write technical reports, the genres, conventions, and vocabularies they use reflect the ideologies of their professions and settings.

The research-driven shift toward this cultural, ideological view of writing creates tensions with the structures and practices that continue to prevail in many educational institutions. The first-year writing requirement, for instance, was historically based on the premise that writing is a universal skill set and singular discourse individuals can master if they are determined and taught well. In this view, literacy is an ideologically neutral tool, a stable, transposable set of codes and conventions that can be acquired and then deployed in virtually any setting. Writing is thus seen as separate from other learning, from ideological differences and struggle, and from the socialization processes that operate in learning environments. Required writing courses and gatekeeping assessments that similarly purport to certify generic literate readiness have been placed at thresholds to higher education based on these assumptions.

The understanding that writing is an ideological, socially involved practice and thus inescapably implicated in identity making has vexed the project of writing education and the institutional structures that facilitate it—like first-year writing and placement tests. In scholarship in rhetoric and composition, much conversation has centered on "academic writing" because educating students to be proficient academic writers continues to be a common goal for postsecondary writing classes. Writing researchers have investigated how institutional projects of teaching academic writing have historically situated students in relation to literacy according to unacknowledged ideological assumptions. When we seek to "apprentice" students into academic writing, what ideological imperatives are being asserted in the ways we choose to conceive of academic writers and writing? Other researchers have positioned writing within sites of complicated ideological exchange and struggle as their research considers writing and writers in relation to diaspora, race, global economics and the consciousnesses, social statuses and embodied histories of writers. This work explores the ways conventions, meanings, power, identities—even notions of the functions and authority of authorship and texts—are culturally produced and socially negotiated.

Among professional educators in writing studies, awareness of writing as ideological enactment has led to efforts to understand and take responsibility for the ideological assumptions and consequences of pedagogical practices.

3.1

WRITING IS LINKED TO IDENTITY

Kevin Roozen

Common perceptions of writing tend to cast it as the act of encoding or inscribing ideas in written form. To view writing in this manner, though, overlooks the roles writing plays in the construction of self. Through writing, writers come to develop and perform identities in relation to the interests, beliefs, and values of the communities they engage with, understanding the possibilities for selfhood available in those communities (see 3.0, "Writing Enacts and Creates Identities and Ideologies"). The act of writing, then, is not so much about using a particular set of skills as it is about becoming a particular kind of person, about developing a sense of who we are.

Our identities are the ongoing, continually under-construction product of our participation in a number of engagements, including those from our near and distant pasts and our potential futures. Given that our participation with our multiple communities involves acting with their texts, writing serves as a key means by which we act with and come to understand the subject matter, the kinds of language, the rhetorical moves, the genres, the media and technologies, and the writing processes and practices at play in our various sites of engagement, as well as the beliefs, values, and interests they reflect (see 1.0, "Writing Is a Social and Rhetorical Activity"). Writing, then, functions as a key form of socialization as we learn to become members of academic disciplines (see 3.4, "Disciplinary and Professional Identities Are Constructed through Writing"), professions, religious groups, community organizations, political parties, families, and so on.

Writing also functions as a means of displaying our identities. Through the writing we do, we claim, challenge, perhaps even contest and resist, our alignment with the beliefs, interests, and values of the communities with which we engage. The extent to which we align ourselves with a particular community, for example, can be gauged by the extent to which we are able and willing to use that community's language, make its rhetorical moves, act with its privileged texts, and participate in its writing processes and practices. As we develop identities aligned with the interests and values of the communities in which we participate, we become more comfortable making the rhetorical and generic moves privileged by those communities.

Understanding the identity work inherent in writing is important for many stakeholders. For teachers and learners, it foregrounds the need to approach writing not simply as a means of learning and using a set of skills, but rather as a means of engaging with the possibilities for selfhood available in a given community. It also means recognizing that the difficulties people have with writing are not necessarily due to a lack of intelligence or a diminished level of literacy but rather to whether they can see themselves as participants in a particular community. For administrators, this threshold concept highlights the demand for structuring the curriculum in ways that allow learners to develop a sense of what it means to become a member of an academic discipline and creating models of assessment that address learners' identity work. For researchers interested in literate activity, it underscores the importance of theoretical perspectives and methodological approaches that make visible the construction of self.

3.2

WRITERS' HISTORIES, PROCESSES, AND IDENTITIES VARY

Kathleen Blake Yancey

Although human beings often seem to share histories, engage in similar composing processes, and have identities that are at the core human, each writer is unique: indeed, each writer is a combination of the collective set of different dimensions and traits and features that make us human.

Writers, developing in the contexts of family, schooling, and culture, continue that development as they write in increasingly multiple and varying contexts—of larger personal relationship structures, in workplace sites, in the civic sphere, and in cultural contexts that themselves are always changing. Initially, as children learning language and writing—a process that continues throughout our lives—people write their ways into a "variety of complex, interwoven social systems" (Brown and Duguid 2000, 140). In the process, each writer begins a lifelong process of balancing individual perspectives and processes with the opportunities, demands, constraints, and genres of specific rhetorical situations and contexts of the larger culture. The ways in which individual writers do this, however, are influenced by their individual histories, processes, and identities.

Writers' identities are, in part, a function of the time when they live: their histories, identities, and processes are situated in a given historical context. Millennia ago, before formal schooling provided instruction in composing, writers employed their own composing processes, drawing on caves, composing hieroglyphics for tombstones, and writing petroglyphs on the walls of canyons. Later, as formal schooling developed in various parts of the world, male children in the upper classes were *instructed* in the art of writing, in the west, for example, learning, in part through a rhetoric keyed to the civic sphere, the five canons of rhetoric: invention, memory, arrangement, style, and delivery. In more recent times, as our knowledge about writing has deepened, we have understood that composing processes also vary according to at least three factors—the individual writer, the genre being composed, and the rhetorical situation. This new knowledge has also shaped understandings about the invention, drafting, reviewing, revising, editing, and publishing of composing. Likewise, although composition has been a school subject in the US university for over a century, the development of models of composing in the 1970s and 1980s, based in the practices of writers, changed the teaching of writing: teachers have shifted from teaching writing through analysis of others' texts to teaching writing through engaging students in composing itself.

Equally important, as composing becomes increasingly digitized and people worldwide learn to compose in multiple spaces and with multiple devices without any formal instruction (Yancey 2004), we are reminded that school is merely one historical context; there are many. In addition, because of the multiple affordances of digital technologies, composers routinely work with images, sounds, and video, as well as with words, to make meaning, and in using these materials to make meaning, individual writers are able to express their own identities and histories.

Writers' identities vary as well, in part through individual and collective identity markers such as gender, race, class, sexual orientation, and physical abilities; in part through individuals' relationships with family and friends; and in part through experiences that both attract and influence identity. Writing itself, especially through genres, also anticipates and, to a certain extent, enforces an identity.

The threshold concept that writers' histories, processes, and identities vary is troublesome because it speaks to the complexity of composing itself and to the complexity of the task of helping students learn to compose. People who want the teaching of writing to be uniform—mapped across grade levels, for instance, with all students inventing in the same way, drafting in the same way, and using the same language—find this threshold concept frustrating, in part because they had hoped a single approach would enfranchise all writers; the failure of such an approach speaks to the differentiation of composing itself given writers' histories and identities. The variation in students' composing processes, like the variation in their histories and identities, thus makes the teaching of writing a complex, sophisticated task. At the same time, it's worth noting the inherently paradoxical nature of writing—that we write as both individuals and as social beings, and that helping writers mature requires helping them write to others while expressing themselves. Put another way, writing is paradoxical because of its provision both for the social and the conventional and for the individual: individuals participating in multiple contexts account for social aspects of writing (see 2.0, "Writing Speaks to Situations through Recognizable Forms," and 4.3, "Learning to Write Effectively Requires Different Kinds of Practice, Time, and Effort"), and at the same time writing is located in an individual who is necessarily distinct (see 4.1, "Text Is an Object Outside of One's Self that Can Be Improved and Developed," and 5.1, "Writing Is an Expression of Embodied Cognition"). In addition, neither writers nor their contexts are static: both change over time, which introduces yet another source of variation and which also means that variation is the normal situation for composing and composers.

3.3

WRITING IS INFORMED BY PRIOR EXPERIENCE

Andrea A. Lunsford

If no one is an island, as poet John Donne famously argued, then no writing is isolated and alone either. Writing is, first of all, always part of a larger netw... or conversation; all writing is in some sense a response to other writing or symbolic action. Even when writing is private or meant for the writer alone, it is shaped by the writer's earlier interactions with writing and with other people and with all the writer has read and learned. Such interactions form a network or conversation that comes from knowledge and from all the experience the writer has had. Here's an example that may help to illuminate this claim: for over two decades, I asked people all over the United States to recall their earliest memories of writing. Many described learning to write their own names: that act seems to signal a significant moment in cognitive and emotional development. But others—left-handers, for example—reported something painful associated with writing: being made to sit on their left hands so they had to write right-handed. Many others spoke of being made to write "I will not X" a hundred times in punishment for some mistake; still others remembered being ridiculed or somehow humiliated for something they had or had not written. For many people, it turned out, prior experience with writing had been negative, and this attitude and these feelings went with them throughout their lives so that they dreaded writing or felt inadequate when faced with a writing task. Luckily, such associations or prior experiences can be mitigated or changed, and that often happens as writers become more confident or encounter more positive experiences with writing. But those early experiences can still linger on.

In addition to drawing on memories of writing, writers also draw on personal knowledge and lived experience in creating new texts (see 2.2, "Genres Are Enacted by Writers and Readers"; 2.3, "Writing Is a Way of Enacting Disciplinarity"; and 2.6, "Texts Get Their Meaning from Other Texts"). Assigned to write an essay, for example, writers summon up the features of an essay they've used in the past or learned about by reading and talking about the essay genre. Likewise, a student writing an argument draws on prior knowledge or experience with producing such a text, including perhaps how to organize an argument for maximum effect. Other writers may draw on something written in the past for a new purpose.

In some instances, prior knowledge and experience are necessary and often helpful; in others they can work against writers. When writers call on strategies they have used before when approaching a new writing task, those strategies may or may not work well in the current situation. In studying college student writers' responses to first-year assignments, for example, Linda Flower found that students tended to rely on a strategy she called "gist and list" (essentially making a point [the gist] and then listing a series of supporting statements) whether that strategy was an effective one or not (Flower et al. 1990). When writers can identify how elements of one writing situation are similar to elements of another, their prior knowledge helps them out in analyzing the current rhetorical situation. But when they simply rely on a strategy or genre or convention out of habit, that prior knowledge may not be helpful at all.

3.4

DISCIPLINARY AND PROFESSIONAL IDENTITIES ARE CONSTRUCTED THROUGH WRITING

Heidi Estrem

While people can negotiate how identities are constructed through writing in a variety of contexts (see 3.1, "Writing Is Linked to Identity"), many first encounter unfamiliar disciplinary (or professional) discourse in college. In most American colleges and universities in the United States, students complete general education courses (introductory courses designed to introduce students to both ways of thinking and disciplinary perspectives within the university) before continuing on to specialized courses within their chosen disciplines or fields. This increasingly discipline-specific learning process involves both the simple acquisition of new knowledge and an "expansion and transformation of identity, of a learner's 'sense of self'" (Meyer and Land 2006, 11). Writing—as a means of thinking, a form of inquiry and research, and a means for communication within a discipline—plays a critical role in that identity transformation and expansion. Disciplines have particular ways of asking and investigating questions enacted through and demonstrated in writing; teachers or researchers demonstrate their memberships in disciplines by using writing in ways validated by disciplines. It is thus through writing that disciplines (and writers [see 2.3, "Writing is a Way of Enacting Disciplinarity"]) are both enacted and encountered by writers—first as students, and then as professionals throughout their careers.

Identities are complex expressions and embodiments of who someone is (see 3.1, "Writing Is Linked to Identity"). For many students in college encountering disciplinary writing for the first time, discipline-specific writing threatens their sense of self because these ways of thinking and writing are so distinct from other more familiar reading and writing practices, such as those valued at home or in other communities in which the students are members (see 3.0, "Writing Enacts and Creates Identities and Ideologies," and 3.5, "Writing Provides a Representation of Ideologies and Identities"). As writers continue to work in the academy and beyond, they negotiate (and challenge) disciplinary identities via writing, finding ways to traverse the differing implicit and explicit writing expectations. The process of learning to manage these tensions contributes to the formation of new identities, for as people progress through their major discipline(s), writing increasingly complex texts in the process, they are also writing themselves into the discipline(s) (see 2.3, "Writing Is a Way of Enacting Disciplinarity"). That process of identity formation is interwoven with learning the writing conventions, practices, habits, and approaches of their discipline.

For many people, the idea that writing is not merely a matter of recording one's research or thoughts, but is in fact a process linked to the development of new, professional identities, is troublesome. Writing can appear to be an act of transcription or representation of processes, not an expression of identity. Many prevalent descriptions of the relationship between writing and research neutralize and generalize disciplinary or professional writing into a last step in the research project, one in which research results are "written up" (see 1.0, "Writing Is a Social and Rhetorical Activity," and 1.1, "Writing Is a Knowledge-Making Activity"). Approaching disciplinary writing as an act of identity and affiliation illuminates how writing in new contexts is not only about learning abstract conventions but also about learning how to *be* within a group with social conventions, norms, and expectations (see 3.0, "Writing Enacts and Creates Identities and Ideologies").

3.5

WRITING PROVIDES A REPRESENTATION
OF IDEOLOGIES AND IDENTITIES

Victor Villanueva

Writing provides a means whereby identities are discovered and constituted. Yet those are never clear cut. We carry many identities, choosing to foreground one (or some) over others depending on the context, the audience, and the rhetorical task at hand (see 3.2, "Writers' Histories, Processes, and Identities Vary"). If I am writing to a school board about a new policy, for example, I will likely foreground my identity as a parent. If I am writing about writing, as I am here, I will foreground my identity as a professor of writing and rhetoric. In like manner, we also carry any number of political identities, identities that reflect particular ideological predispositions. We can write as a liberal or a conservative, as a woman recognizing particular power dynamics, as a person of color. Identity politics—the idea that one's self-defined identities drive one's choices as they engage in discussions, actions, and interactions—entails a conscious decision by the individual to enter into what critical theorist Gyatri Spivak (1987) terms a "strategic essentialism," a reduction of complex political and economic relations in order to present a political statement.

Identity politics tends toward the construction of a single identity. But we know that identit*ies* are multifaceted. One can be liberal on social issues but a conservative on fiscal issues. None of us is ideologically "pure." Or one can be a gay man of color, wherein sets of different conflicts and different power relations can occur. Even as there is a great deal of value to identity politics, then, when writing from an overtly political or cultural position there is a risk in identity politics of reducing cultures, races, ethnicities, genders, sexualities, or class relations to their "natures," especially when writers do this as they imagine their audiences and their identities.

There are limits to what can be anticipated about what readers know, assume, or believe. To write from the position of one who is "color blind," for example, could be read as a denial of complex histories and current hierarchical differences in power and economic relations. To write about a gay relationship in terms of husbands and wives is to maintain conventional conceptions of gender roles. In other words, because all writing is inflected by power dynamics shaped by identities and ideologies, writers must become aware of the how those identities and ideologies are represented in their writing.

Compositionist James Berlin (1987) points to a way in which representation can be brought into the writing classroom. In his taxonomies
of epistemological assumptions about writing, he provides essentially
three conceptions of how writing can be seen to work: as reflective, a
mirror of an objective reality; as intentional, conveying what an author
intends so that the reader's job is to discern that intention; or as or constructed, so that there is a negotiation within the writer with his or her
ways of seeing the world and a negotiation within the reader between
his or her own worldviews and the perceived worldviews of the writer.
Students (maybe even most nonspecialists) accept the first two assumptions, that writing is transparent and/or that it conveys exactly what a
writer meant to say. A "pedagogy of representation" (Giroux 1994) dis-
rupts these two perceptions and asks students to do the critical work of
discovering the kinds of cultural, political, and economic assumptions
contained within their own writing and within popular culture. Guiding
questions would be what's being said? and what's left unsaid? These two
simple questions can begin to uncover the power dynamics contained
in all writing.

References

Bakhtin, M. M. . 1986. *Speech Genres and Other Late Essays*. Austin: University of Texas
    Press.
Berlin, James. 1987. *Rhetoric and Reality*. Carbondale: Southern Illinois University Press.
Brown, John Seely, and Paul Duguid. 2000. *The Social Life of Information*. Boston, MA:
    Harvard Business School Press.
Flower, Linda, Victoria Stein, John Ackerman, Margaret J. Kantz, Kathleen McCormick,
    and Wayne C. Peck. 1990. *Reading-to-Write: Exploring a Cognitive and Social Process*. New
    York: Oxford University Press.
Gee, James Paul. 2008. *Social Linguistics and Literacies: Ideology in Discourses*. 3rd ed. New
    York: Routledge.
Giroux, Henry A. 1994. "Living Dangerously: Identity Politics and the New Cultural
    Racism." In *Between Borders: Pedagogy and the Politics of Cultural Studies*, edited by Henry
    A. Giroux and Peter McLaren, 1–27. New York: Routledge.
Meyer, Jan H. F., and Ray Land. 2006. *Overcoming Barriers to Student Understanding:
    Threshold Concepts and Troublesome Knowledge*. London: Routledge.
Spivak, Giyatri. 1987. *In Other Worlds: Essays in Cultural Politics*. London: Taylor and
    Francis.
Vygotsky, L. S. 1978. *Mind in Society: The Development of Higher Psychological Processes*.
    Cambridge: Harvard University Press.
Yancey, Kathleen Blake. 2004. "Made Not Only in Words: Composition in a New Key."
    College Composition and Communication 56 (2): 297–328. http://dx.doi.org/10.2307
    /4140651.

CONCEPT 4
All Writers Have More to Learn

4.0

ALL WRITERS HAVE MORE TO LEARN
Shirley Rose

Many people assume that all writing abilities can be learned once and for always. However, although writing is learned, all writers always have more to learn about writing.

The ability to write is not an innate trait humans are born possessing. Humans are "symbol-using (symbol-making, symbol-misusing) animals," and writing is symbolic action, as Kenneth Burke has explained (Burke 1966, 16). Yet learning to write requires conscious effort, and most writers working to improve their effectiveness find explicit instruction in writing to be more helpful than simple trial and error without the benefit of an attentive reader's response. Often, one of the first lessons writers learn, one that may be either frustrating or inspiring, is that they will never have learned all that can be known about writing and will never be able to demonstrate all they do know about writing.

Writers soon discover that writing strategies that are effective for them in one context are often inappropriate and ineffective in another context in which they need or want to write; even when strategies work, writers still struggle to figure out what they want to say and how to say it. They struggle because writing is not just transcribing preformed ideas but also developing new ones; thus a writer never becomes a perfect writer who already knows how to write anything and everything. This difficulty and imperfectability of writing, and the fact that it is not a "natural" phenomenon (see 1.6, "Writing Is Not Natural") is one reason formal writing instruction is typical of schooling in the United States at all levels. But learning about writing doesn't happen only in school. For example, James Gee (2004) showed how a teenage writer of fan fiction learned about writing outside school through the practice, advice, and modeling provided by her online community of other writers. Likewise, instruction in writing does not necessarily end when formal schooling ends. Writers encounter new

DOI: 10.7330/9781607325789.c004

contexts, genres, tasks, and audiences as they move among workplaces and communities beyond formal schooling, and these new contexts call for new kinds of writing.

With experience, writers do discover that some writing habits developed in one context can be helpful in another. For example, habits such as writing multiple drafts or setting aside regular, frequent periods for writing in a place free of distractions often prove effective regardless of the writing task or context. Likewise, writing strategies useful in one context, such as using explicit transitional words to signal organization or using illustrations to develop an idea, will work well in many different writing contexts for many different purposes. However, these same writing habits and strategies will not work in all writing situations (see 5.3, "Habituated Practice Can Lead to Entrenchment"). There is no such thing as "writing in general"; therefore, there is no one lesson about writing that can make writing good in all contexts (see 2.0, "Writing Speaks to Situations through Recognizable Forms," and 2.2, "Genres Are Enacted by Writers and Readers"). Writers must struggle to write in new contexts and genres, a matter of transferring what they know but also learning new things about what works in the present situation. The difficulty of drawing on prior knowledge in this way has spawned a thread of research transfer of knowledge about writing (see Wardle 2012). The working knowledge that enables a writer to select the practices and strategies appropriate for a particular writing context and task is learned over time through experience as a writer and as a reader of writing. Therefore, a demonstration of one's ability to write effectively in one context cannot constitute proof of one's ability to write in other contexts.

Writers—and teachers of writing—might sometimes wish all writing abilities could be learned once and for always, just as one can learn how to spell a particular word correctly or how to punctuate a quotation correctly once and for always. However, many writing abilities, such as choosing the most appropriate and precise word, and exercising good judgment in deciding whether to quote directly or to paraphrase in any given writing situation, cannot be learned just once. This imperfectability of writing ability is even more evident when a writer must learn how to choose and use evidence to make an effective argument in an unfamiliar situation.

This threshold concept can be difficult to understand because the content of most school subjects is divided into categories and levels of difficulty and sequenced in a way that assumes students must learn the content or skills of one level or stage before moving on to the next level. Unlike these subjects, formal writing instruction is usually designed to repeat the same principles or lessons over and over as student writers encounter new situations for writing and learning.

This is an important threshold concept for educators to understand because it enables us to recognize that it is impossible to make a valid judgment of a student writer's ability by examining a single sample of his or her writing, particularly a sample of writing that does not address a specific rhetorical situation (see 1.7, "Assessing Writing Shapes Contexts and Instruction"). For these same reasons, one cannot assume that a student who has demonstrated the ability to write a literary critical analysis of *Romeo and Juliet* as a senior in high school will also be able to write a paper outlining issues currently being discussed in response to new developments in research on childhood diabetes for a college course.

This threshold concept is helpful for all writers to understand because it will enable them to recognize that encountering difficulty in a writing situation is an indication that they are ready to learn something new about writing.

Writers never cease learning to write, never completely perfect their writing ability, as long as they encounter new or unfamiliar life experiences that require or inspire writing.

4.1

TEXT IS AN OBJECT OUTSIDE OF ONESELF THAT CAN BE IMPROVED AND DEVELOPED

Charles Bazerman and Howard Tinberg

In the course of writing, whether preliminary notes, a sketch, or a full draft, a writer inscribes signs that now exist on paper, digital display, or some other medium. While these signs may have their origin in meanings within the mind of the writer and the initial spontaneous choice of words, they now have been externalized into an independent artifact that can be examined, revised, or otherwise worked on by the writer, collaborators, or other people.

For writers, this externalization decreases the amount of material they must remember and attend to while composing (reducing cognitive load) and allows them to focus attention on limited issues. Externalization also allows writers to look at the text produced so far to see how clearly it reads, what it conveys, whether it can be improved in any way. This working on a text now external to the writer allows a more technical examination, distancing the writer from an idealized sense of meaning and what they feel internally in order to see what the words actually convey. The writer potentially can take the part of the reader. This distancing, however, is not automatic, as the writer may assume the words convey all that they imagine. Thus, becoming aware that the text exists outside the writer's projection and must convey meaning to readers is an important threshold in developing a more professional attitude toward the act of writing and what is produced. Insofar as writers see the text as not yet fulfilling initial ambitions, they can work to improve the text to convey as much as their technical skill and craft allow.

Collaborators, team members, supervisors, editors, and others who may share the work of producing text do not share the initial writer's attachment to the anticipated meaning and have only what the inscribed words bring; they thus provide better measures of what the text actually conveys. While they may view the text with a cooler eye, noting its limitations and failures to convey, they also may lack a sense of all the text may become and of the initial author's intentions. The emerging and changing text then becomes a site of negotiated work to produce the final document.

In response to the view that writing is expressionistic—revealing primarily writers' thoughts and emotions—composition scholars have over the last several decades promoted a view of writing as socially constructed, "crowd-sourced" we'd say these days (Flower 1994; Gere 1987; LeFevre 1987; Lunsford and Ede 1990). More fundamentally, this view is an extension of George Herbert Mead's (1934) understanding that we form our sense of the self through taking the part of the other in our struggle to make ourselves understood. Such a view, while no longer positing that the author is dead, does encourage us to see the text as existing independently of the author and thus capable of being changed and perfected by the author and others.

4.2

FAILURE CAN BE AN IMPORTANT PART OF WRITING DEVELOPMENT

Collin Brooke and Allison Carr

It may seem counterintuitive to suggest that the teaching of writing should focus as much on puzzling out failure as it does on rewarding success. We often forget, however, that successful writers aren't those who are simply able to write brilliant first drafts; often, the writing we encounter has been heavily revised and edited and is sometimes the result of a great deal of failure (see 4.4, "Revision Is Central to Developing Writing," and 4.3, "Learning to Write Effectively Requires Different Kinds of Practice, Time, and Effort"). As renowned writer

Anne Lamott observes, "Almost all good writing begins with terrible first efforts. You need to start somewhere" (Lamott 1995, 303).

As students progress throughout their educational careers and the expectations for their writing evolve from year to year and sometimes course to course, there is no way we can expect them to be able to intuit these shifting conditions. They must have the opportunity to try, to fail, and to learn from those failures as a means of intellectual growth. Edward Burger (2012), professor of mathematics and coauthor of *The 5 Elements of Effective Thinking*, explains that "in reality, every idea from every discipline is a human idea that comes from a natural, thoughtful, and (ideally) unending journey in which thinkers deeply understand the current state of knowledge, take a tiny step in a new direction, almost immediately hit a dead end, learn from that misstep, and, through iteration, inevitably move forward."

In the writing classroom, when assessment is tied too completely to final products, students are more likely to avoid risking failure for fear of damaging their grades, and this fear works against the learning process. They focus instead on what the teacher wants and simply hope to be able to get it right on the first try. Burger (2012) advocates building "quality of failure" into his courses and reports that his students are willing to take greater risks and to examine their missteps for what they can change about them.

One of the most important things students can learn is that failure is an opportunity for growth. As sites of language development, writing classrooms, especially, should make space for quality of failure, or what Lamott describes as "shitty first drafts," by treating failure as something all writers work through, rather than as a symptom of inadequacy or stupidity. Writers need the time and space to explore Thomas Edison's proverbial ten thousand ways that won't work in order to find the ways that do. Such practices will enable writing teachers and students to develop a healthy dialogue around the experience of failure, perhaps leading to the development of what we might call *pedagogies of failure*, or ways of teaching that seek to illuminate the myriad ways writing gets done by examining all the ways it doesn't. Embracing failure in the writing classroom in these ways makes failure speakable and doable.

Outside of the classroom, the capacity for failure (and thus success) is one of the most valuable abilities a writer can possess. The ability to write well comes neither naturally nor easily; the thinkers we praise and admire are not the lucky few born with innate talent. Rather, they are the ones who are able to make mistakes, learn from them, and keep writing until they get it right. J. K. Rowling (2008), for example, is quite open about how she "failed on an epic scale" before she was able to write the *Harry Potter* series. In her 2008 commencement address at Harvard University, she explained, "It is impossible to live without failing at something, unless you live so cautiously that you might as well not have lived at all—in which case, you fail by default."

4.3

LEARNING TO WRITE EFFECTIVELY REQUIRES DIFFERENT KINDS OF PRACTICE, TIME, AND EFFORT

Kathleen Blake Yancey

When someone wants to swim, they get into the water: if we want to write, we put pen to paper, fingers to keyboard, or fingertips to touch screen.

Through practice, we become familiar with writing; it becomes part of us. What we practice is who we are; if we want to be writers, we need to write. And in the practice of writing, we develop writing capacities, among them the ability to adjust and adapt to different contexts, purposes, and audiences.

One kind of practice provides fluidity. Much like a swimmer becoming familiar with the water, writers become familiar with writing—with the feel of a pen in the hand; with the sense of putting individual words on a page that then come together to form larger blocks of meaning, whether sentences, paragraphs, full texts; and with the habit of reviewing what we have just written to see how it fits with what we thought we were writing and with what it is we thought we wanted to say and to share—whether, from our perception, the writing will speak to situations and contexts using conventions of a genre and medium we recognize and think our audience(s) will, too (see 2.0, "Writing Speaks to Situations through Recognizable Forms").

Another kind of practice can refine technique, whether that be dialogue in a narrative, citations for a scientific research paper, or a rhetorical appeal to an elected official. With practice, we can create what seems otherwise out of reach or totally foreign, can compose a text—of words or of words and other elements—shaped by and in response to context. Practice can focus on the whole of a composing process or on different aspects of composing: inventing, researching, drafting, revising, sharing, editing, and publishing.

Practice can involve writing in different spaces, with different materials, and with different technologies. Some writers prefer to write at the same time of day in the same location; others like to change locations;

some like to compose with the same pencil or in the same writer's note-book. As digital technologies have become ubiquitous, writers have become more aware of all technologies, from a pen designed for cal-ligraphy on a piece of fine paper to the dynamic touch screen of a cell-phone, and the ways these affordances may influence writing. Likewise, writers necessarily also work in multiple modalities—whether the modal-ity be on the page through document design or on the networked screen bringing words, images, videos, and sound into a single text. In an age when so many spaces and affordances are available, writers need considerable practice keyed not only to fluidity and technique but also to differentiated practice across different spaces of writing, working with different technologies of writing.

Practice can also involve other people, who can help us see what is working in a text and what is not; with their responses, we can revise so as to communicate more clearly. In school, organized around disci-plines, practices can vary, and this is yet another sense of the word *prac-tice*: a set of recurring activities located in a specific community. The practice of writing a poem may require no research; the practice of com-pleting a research project in anthropology may require research in the field, and research in the library as the project is being drafted. These practices support participation in different areas of inquiry, themselves situated in what Jean Lave and Etienne Wenger call "communities of practice" (Lave and Wenger 2000).

The threshold concept that learning to write effectively, especially in different contexts or communities of practice, takes different kinds of practice, and such practice takes time and effort, is troublesome for three reasons. First, writers are often assumed simply to be "born": that is, a good writer is assumed to be a good writer "naturally" (see 1.6, "Writing Is Not Natural," and 4.0, "All Writers Have More to Learn"). In this view of writing, the amount and kind of practice is irrelevant and superfluous because practice would make no difference. Second, some people believe that when we learn to write in one genre, we have learned to write in all; but to write in any genre, we need practice in that genre and in the con-ventions defining that genre. Third, this threshold concept locates writing specifically as a practice situated within communities, which suggests how complex writing is and how, as an activity, it spans a lifetime.

Research has demonstrated that for effective writers and writing, practice is the key: engaging in the different kinds of practices identified above—to acquire fluency, to focus on techniques and strategies, and to engage with other humans—is the way for all human beings to develop into competent writers.

4.4

REVISION IS CENTRAL TO DEVELOPING WRITING

Doug Downs

To create the best possible writing, writers work iteratively, composing in a number of versions, with time between each for reflection, reader feedback, and/or collaborator development. The revision implied in this process—that is, significant development of a text's ideas, structure, and/or design—is central to developing writing. (*Revision* here is distinct from line editing or copyediting to "polish" a text.) In the same way that writing is not perfectible, writing also is not in the category of things that are often right the first time (see 5.1, "Writing Is an Expression of Embodied Cognition"). This principle also implies two corollaries. First, unrevised writing (especially more extended pieces of writing) will rarely be as well suited to its purpose as it could be with revision. Second, writers who don't revise are likely to see fewer positive results from their writing than those who build time for feedback and revision into their writing workflows. When we teach the centrality of revision to writing development, therefore, we must also teach writers to develop workflows that anticipate and rely on revision and to discover what methods of revision best suit their own writing processes.

Revision works because writing shares a characteristic of other language-based endeavors: using language not only represents one's existing ideas, it tends to generate additional language and ideas (see 3.0, "Writing Enacts and Creates Identities and Ideologies"). Writing something usually gives the writer something new, more, or different to say. Therefore, while writing, writers usually find something to say that they didn't have to say before writing. This phenomenon creates an effect analogous to driving with headlights. The headlights reach only a fraction of the way to the destination; a writer can only begin writing what they "see" at the beginning. Driving to the end of the headlights' first reach—writing the first draft—lets the headlights now illuminate the next distance ahead. A writer at the end of their first draft now sees things they did not when they began, letting them "drive on" through another draft by writing what they would have said had they known at the beginning of the first draft what they now know at the end of it (see 4.1, "Text Is an Object Outside of One's Self that Can Be Improved and Developed").

From another angle, revision works by building into the textual-production process time and space for further consideration of a writing problem by the writer, for garnering additional perspectives from other readers and collaborating writers, and for review of a draft against specific criteria (e.g., the directness of a claim or the strength of evidence for it). The expectation of revision—the building of time into a writing process (see 4.3, "Learning to Write Effectively Requires Different Kinds of Practice, Time, and Effort")—creates both the opportunity for, and sometimes directed prompting for, looking at the text again, differently.

The threshold concept that revision is central to developing writing can be difficult in a number of ways. Novice or unreflective writers, especially students, may see revision as punishment for poor performance. Being told to write again or write more, especially if the assigned writing has little intrinsic value to the writer or is used primarily to judge them, may hardly seem like a positive opportunity. Teachers may heighten this effect by making revision optional (rather than every bit as expected a phase of the writer's workflow as drafting) and even reserving the option only for weak pieces of writing. ("I let them revise if they get a low grade.") Students, teachers, writers, and educational policymakers must understand the implication of this threshold concept: revising, or the need to revise, is not an indicator of poor writing or weak writers but much the opposite—a sign and a function of skilled, mature, professional writing and craft.

4.5

ASSESSMENT IS AN ESSENTIAL COMPONENT OF LEARNING TO WRITE

Peggy O'Neill

Assessment is often associated with external mandates and formal accountability systems. Yet, assessment is also a critical component of writing and learning to write. Assessment conceived of in this way is not about grades, exams, or standardized tests but rather about teaching and learning (Shepard 2000). In writing, it is essential for writers to learn to assess texts written by others as well as their own work—both the processes used to create the texts and products that result. Brian Huot calls this pedagogical approach "instructive evaluation" and explains that it "involves the student in the process of evaluation, making her aware of what it is she is trying to create" and it "requires that we involve the student in all phases of the assessment of her work" (Huot 2002, 69).

In this sense, assessment is essential in all stages of the writing process. Through the prewriting, drafting, revision, editing, and publishing of a text, writers assess various components of the rhetorical situation as well as a variety of texts (their own and, frequently, others'). They must assess options and make decisions based on those assessments. For example, writers assess the situation to determine the purpose of the writing, its audience(s), and the context. They select the appropriate genre, writing technology, and publishing medium (see 2.2, "Genres Are Enacted by Writers and Readers," and 2.4, "All Writing Is Multimodal"). Writers must also evaluate their own processes. They may need to examine their approaches to a task, such as searching for information, to determine if it is effective or if a different approach would be more productive (e.g., Is this database useful for my topic? Am I using the appropriate search terms?). Writers must also assess feedback on writing, asking whether suggestions are useful and how they might respond. Once texts are drafted, a writer must assess the product, considering issues such as the appropriateness of style and content, the persuasiveness of evidence, the extent to which conventions of grammar and usage have been followed. Writers also assess texts written by others: for accuracy, legitimacy, and bias, for genre conventions, or for the audience's expectations.

To learn and improve, writers need to develop assessment abilities; therefore, students benefit when teachers integrate assessment throughout the learning process through a variety of activities. These assessment activities can be open, fluid, and tentative (Huot 2002), as in feedback on an early draft that may include a few critical questions or a conversation in which the writer explains why they made a particular choice. The assessment activities may also be more formalized, such as a structured protocol for a self-assessment of a text. By teaching students how to assess both the product and processes of their work, writing teachers are helping students prepare for future writing tasks and opportunities.

4.6

WRITING INVOLVES THE NEGOTIATION OF LANGUAGE DIFFERENCES

Paul Kei Matsuda

All writing entails language—or more specifically, the internalized knowledge of words, phrases, and sentences and how they are put together to create meaning. This statement may seem obvious to some. Yet, language is often taken for granted in the discussion of writing, especially when writers and writing teachers assume that all writers share more or less the same intuitive knowledge of language structures and functions—a condition described by Paul Kei Matsuda as the "myth of linguistic homogeneity" (Matsuda 2006). In reality, however, the knowledge of language held by individual language users varies. No one is a perfect language user, and writers from distinct sociolinguistic contexts (i.e., regional, socioeconomic, ethnic) often come with notice-ably different language features in their heads—and in their writing. Furthermore, in today's globalized world, where the audience for writing is increasingly multilingual and multinational, it is more important than ever to see the negotiation of language as an integral part of all writing activities.

As writers strive to use a shared code that allows for effective commu-nication, it is important for all writers and readers to develop the aware-ness that we are all participating in the process of negotiating language differences. In any writing context, the audience will likely include translingual individuals—those who grew up using different varieties of the target language or another language altogether. For this reason, language features (e.g., vocabulary, idioms, sentence structures) as well as rhetorical features (e.g., persuasive appeals, cultural references and reader-writer positioning) that were once unmarked may need to be negotiated by writers and writing teachers. For instance, writers cannot assume that the phrase *to beat a dead horse* will be understood by all read-ers universally; to be effective, writers may need to consider embedding contextual clues or even building in some redundancies.

By the same token, readers and writing teachers cannot assume that what were once considered errors are indeed errors; they may reflect language practices perfectly acceptable in some parts of the world— or even in different parts of the same country. For example, including some Spanish words or phrases into sentences is perfectly acceptable for an audience of English-Spanish bilingual writers or users of English-Spanish contact varieties—as long as they do not violate the language rules shared by both users. For a mixed audience that includes non-Spanish users (which is often the case in international academic writ-ing), writers may need to provide additional information (translation, footnote, etc.) in order to facilitate the rhetorical goal of writing (see 1.0, "Writing Is a Social and Rhetorical Activity").

This renewed realization about the changing nature of language and the presence of language differences has several implications. Teachers who use writing as part of their instruction must develop an understand-ing of the nature of language, principles of language development, and language features situated in various contexts of use. Such knowl-edge is especially important in facilitating the development of commu-nicative competence (Bachman 1990) among writers who come from nondominant language backgrounds. Teachers also must become more aware of the fuzzy boundary between appropriate usage and inappropriate usage (i.e., errors) to help students understand when and how language differences become negotiable. To help students negotiate language differences successfully—including making principled decisions about whether or not to adopt dominant language practices—teachers must understand various strategies for negotiating language differences. Finally, teachers must help students understand the risks involved in negotiating language differences. Beyond the classroom, all writers today need to fully understand the diversity within a language as well as how languages continue to change.

References

Bachman, Lyle. 1990. *Fundamental Considerations in Language Testing*. Oxford: University of Oxford Press.

Burger, Edward. 2012. "Teaching to Fail." *Inside Higher Ed*, August 21. https://www.inside highered.com/views/2012/08/21/essay-importance-teaching-failure.

Burke, Kenneth. 1966. *Language as Symbolic Action*. Berkeley: University of California Press.

Flower, Linda. 1994. *The Construction of Negotiated Meaning: A Social Cognitive Theory of Writing*. Carbondale: Southern Illinois University Press.

Gee, James Paul. 2004. *Situated Language and Learning: A Critique of Traditional Schooling*. New York: Routledge.

Gere, Ann Ruggles. 1987. *Writing Groups: History, Theory, and Implications*. Carbondale: Southern Illinois University Press.

Huot, Brian. 2002. *(Re)Articulating Writing Assessment for Teaching and Learning*. Logan: Utah State University Press.

Lamott, Anne. 1995. *Bird by Bird: Some Instructions on Writing and Life*. New York: Anchor Books.

Lave, Jean, and Etienne Wenger. 2000. *Communities of Practice*. Cambridge: Cambridge University Press.

LeFevre, Karen Burke. 1987. *Invention as a Social Act*. Carbondale: Southern Illinois University Press.

Lunsford, Andrea, and Lisa Ede. 1990. *Singular Texts/Plural Authors*. Carbondale: Southern Illinois University Press.

Matsuda, Paul Kei. 2006. "The Myth of Linguistic Homogeneity in U.S. College Composition." *College English* 68 (6): 637–51. http://dx.doi.org/10.2307/25472180.

Mead, George Herbert. 1934. *Mind, Self, and Society: From the Standpoint of a Social Behaviorist*. Chicago: University of Chicago Press.

Rowling, J. K. 2008. "The Fringe Benefits of Failure, and the Importance of Imagination." *Harvard Magazine*. http://harvardmagazine.com/2008/06/the-fringe-benefits-failure-the-importance-imagination.

Shepard, Lorrie A. 2000. "The Role of Assessment in a Learning Culture." *Educational Researcher* 29 (7): 4–14. http://dx.doi.org/10.3102/0013189X029007004.

Wardle, Elizabeth. 2012. "Understanding 'Transfer' from FYC: Preliminary Results of a Longitudinal Study." *WPA: Writing Program Administration* 31 (1/2): 6–85.

CONCEPT 5
Writing Is (Also Always) a Cognitive Activity

5.0

WRITING IS (ALSO ALWAYS) A COGNITIVE ACTIVITY
Dylan B. Dryer

Behind the claim by Linda Adler-Kassner and Elizabeth Wardle in "Metaconcept: Writing Is an Activity and a Subject of Study" in this volume that "writing can never be anything but a social and rhetorical act" are decades of research inspired by what is now known as the *social turn*. Those applying insights from the social turn to the study of writing found again and again that any act of writing is situated in complex activity systems that enmesh any writer's motives with other spaces, traditions, values, ideologies, other humans, previous iterations of the genre, and the constraints and affordances of language itself (see 1.5, "Writing Mediates Activity"; 2.1, "Writing Represents the World, Events, Ideas, and Feelings"; 2.3, "Writing Is a Way of Enacting Disciplinarity"; and 3.2, "Writers' Histories, Processes, and Identities Vary"). But if writing is always a social and rhetorical act, it necessarily involves cognition. While contemporary advanced research on writing is profoundly and productively oriented to influences on writing outside the skull, as it were, the four concepts in this chapter signal the beginnings of a convergence as potentially transformative as the "social turn" itself (after all, the "social turn" was in part a rejection of prior attempts to conceptualize writing as a solely cognitive phenomenon). To see this potential clearly, we must revisit what is known about composing processes inside the skull.

Well before the social turn, writing researchers in the late 1960s were examining cognitive aspects of writing, and their work became particularly relevant to those teaching in the open-admissions campuses of the 1970s. Many students came to those campuses with writing experiences and composing strategies that perplexed and dismayed their instructors; some faculty declared that many of these students could not write at all (for more on this era, see Bizzell 1982; Lu 1999;

DOI: 10.7330/9781607325789.c005

Soliday 2002). Even as some faculty members and researchers attributed students' writing struggles to mental and even cultural "deficits," others were trying to map mental processes in a more descriptive way (Flower and Hayes 1981; Perl 1979). By observing writers who had been asked to verbalize what they were thinking while they were drafting and revising, these researchers found evidence for a writing process that extends before and after the moment of text production. The models these researchers produced helped break the grip of still-dominant assumptions that writing was simply a matter of transcribing thought while avoiding error (for more on this, see 1.4, "Words Get Their Meaning from Other Words" and 1.9, "Writing Is a Technology through Which Writers Create and Recreate Meaning"). Researchers in cognition and writing attempted to diagnose and develop interventions for issues still important today: What makes writers "blocked," or causes them to stall once they get going? What can writers do to overcome anxiety? Why do writers interrupt higher-order attempts to shape meaning to correct lower-order issues of spelling and punctuation, and does it matter? What happens when writers' plans for the texts they hope to produce or the readers they hope to reach are changed by the texts they've already produced? What are writers *doing* when they pause while writing? Is there a relationship between syntactical complexity and "maturity" of thought? How do the strategies of skilled writers differ from those of novices? Can thinking *about* thinking enhance writing, reading, and/or revision practices? All of these questions are about cognition although, as previous threshold concepts demonstrated, we know they are not only about cognition.

This early cognitive research produced findings that continue to underpin our field's beliefs and activities. For example, anxiety (about error, imagined audience, or perfectionism) can overwhelm composing processes and can be mitigated with low-stakes, generative writing (Bloom 1981; Elbow   31; Rose 1985); revision strategies depend on what writers think revision is (Bridwell 1980; Sommers 1980); composing and revising processes are malleable and genre specific (Britton et al. 1975); composing practices can transform as well as transcribe knowledge (Bereiter and Scardamalia 1987); and, perhaps most generally, the ways people think about approaching a writing task affect their experiences with it.

Researchers in the cognitive sciences who happen to study writing have independently and empirically validated much of that early work: neural processes essential to writing must be successfully coordinated across different areas of the brain; revision, even for seemingly uncomplicated "errors," is cognitively quite complex; and writers' syntactical fluency improves in tight correspondence with knowledge of their topics. Perhaps most important, writers' brains have structural limitations on what is known as *working memory*—where fleeting and mutable bits of information, images, to-do lists, or immediate plans are held, juggled, and discarded. Unfortunately, working memory appears to be fairly inelastic and zero-sum. This limitation is why unfamiliar task loads (as alluded to in 1.6, "Writing Is Not Natural") can reduce performance in other, usually high-competency, areas; why rates of surface error rise predictably when students attempt a new genre for the first time (see also Quinlan et al. 2012); and why field researchers find writers creatively rigging up makeshift additional capacity for their working memories (Angeli 2015; Barber et al. 2006; MacKay 1999).

What's more, there is now substantial evidence that composing practices measurably influence other mental processes (recall, goal setting, attention span, knowledge acquisition, processing time, etc.) as well as psychosocial and even *physiological* phenomena (stress and anxiety levels, recovery from trauma, immunological response, pain sensitivity, postoperative recovery, etc.). As 5.1 ("Writing Is an Expression of Embodied Cognition") makes clear, writing is cognitive not only because it "draws on the full resources of our nervous system" but because it actively influences our nervous system as well (Berninger and Richards 2012; Berninger and Winn 2006). Evidently, as Marilyn Cooper argues in a review of recent work in neurophenomenology, what we write literally helps make us who we are (Cooper 2011, 443). This phenomenon helps explain why writers constrained to "repeated practice of the same genres" may, as explained in 5.3, become "entrenched" in particular approaches or conventions. Although neuroplasticity (the capacity of the brain to create and reinforce new neural connections through learning and use) is only now becoming part of the conversation in US writing studies, our most progressive composition pedagogies have long emphasized metacognition and reflection for just this reason. That is, not only do compositionists want writers to "demonstrate consciousness of process that will enable them to reproduce success" (see 5.3, "Habituated Practice Can Lead to Entrenchment") and to "begin assessing themselves as writers, recognizing and building on their prior knowledge about writing" (see 5.4, "Reflection Is Critical for Writers' Development"), they hope to ensure that writers receiving instruction in one context are also equipped to fend off the cognitive entrenchment of repetition and overgeneralization.

As long as teachers keep this caution about entrenchment in mind, working memory and the benefits of automaticity are set to become powerful enabling concepts for modern writing studies. All writers can increase fluency and performance through naturalizing routines; just as letter shapes recede from children's consciousness (or more specifically, the frontal lobes) and free up working memory for higher-order composing goals, so too will even the most structurally elaborate academic and workplace genres eventually become assimilated into writers' routines (see 2.1, "Writing Represents the World, Events, Ideas, and Feelings"). Teachers and supervisors alike should remember that automaticity takes time, perhaps at a temporary cost to other skill sets (see 4.2, "Failure Can Be an Important Part of Writing Development," and 4.3, "Learning to Write Effectively Requires Different Kinds of Practice, Time, and Effort") and that writers taking on a new task are attempting to forge neurological connections that literally *aren't there yet* (see James and Engelhardt 2012; Richards et al. 2011).

In sum, insights from the social turn and insights from what some are calling the *neurological turn* appear to be converging, as can be seen in this recent definition from two cognitive researchers: "The writing process is supported by a single system—the writer's internal mind-brain interacting with the external environment (including technology tools)" (Berninger and Winn 2006, 108).

5.1

WRITING IS AN EXPRESSION OF EMBODIED COGNITION
Charles Bazerman and Howard Tinberg

Writing is a full act of the mind, drawing on the full resources of our nervous system, formulating communicative impulses into thoughts and words, and transcribing through the work of the fingers. Writers at the computer or desk carry the tension of thought throughout their full posture, can grimace at the difficult contradiction, and can burst into laughter at the surprising discovery or the pleasure of an elegant phrase.

This is as true of the reasoned and evidence-grounded academic writer as of the impassioned writer of love letters. The emotional engagement of scientific writers for their subject may entail careful attention to evidence and reasoning grounded in prior work in the field and an understanding of the theory and methodological principles of the field; yet without a passion for the subject that turns a writer's full mind and thought to the task of producing new words and ideas, little of value would get written.

If cognition assumes complex mental processes at work, then embodied cognition draws in addition upon the physical and affective aspects of the composing process. While there is still much to learn about how the brain and mind work when engaged in the complex task of writing, it was evident to theorists as early as James Moffett (1968) and Ann Berthoff (1978; 1981) that writing comes from full engagement of the entire writer, which is developed across many years of a developing self. Both drew on the work of Lev Vygotsky (1986) who, in the early years of the twentieth century, explored the role of language internalization and externalization in the social formation of mind and emotions (see Bazerman 2012). More recently, psychologists such as Ron Kellogg (2008) have documented the extensive concentration and long time it takes a writer to develop. Howard Gardner (2008) as well has called for recognition of the full, human dimension of both readers and writers in the construction of meaning. Finally, a number of teachers drawing on psychoanalytic traditions have considered how writing challenges and exposes elements of emotions and psychological structures (e.g., Alcorn 2002).

5.2

METACOGNITION IS NOT COGNITION
Howard Tinberg

"Do you know your knowledge?" asks Samuel Taylor Coleridge, trying to point out the difference between knowing what we know and knowing that we know (qtd. in Berthoff 1978, 233). The first calls upon cognition while the second requires metacognition. In other words, to think through a solution to a problem differs from an awareness of how we came to resolve that problem, or, as Kara Taczak notes in this collection, writers engage in cognition when they reflect on "what they are doing in that particular moment" but display metacognition when they consider "why they made the rhetorical choices they did" (78). For those of us who teach writing, the objective is not just to have our students produce effective writing—that is, to respond in logical and thoughtful ways to the question posed. We also want our students to demonstrate consciousness of process that will enable them to reproduce success. Metacognition is not cognition. Performance, however thoughtful, is not the same as awareness of how that performance came to be.

Cognition refers to the acquisition and application of knowledge through complex mental processes. Writers draw upon cognitive processes when they

- demonstrate an understanding of the question;
- deploy accurately and purposefully concepts, knowledge sets, and terms that reveal genuine expertise;
- meet the needs of their audience;
- fulfill the requirements of genre; or
- exhibit a control over language, grammar, and mechanics.

But the effective accomplishment of writing tasks over time requires even more. It calls upon metacognition, or the ability to perceive the very steps by which success occurs and to articulate the various qualities and components that contribute in significant ways to the production of effective writing, such as

- discerning the structure of a draft;
- delineating patterns of error; or
- discriminating between what is necessary in a draft and what in the end serves little purpose.

Metacognition requires that writers think about their mental processes. Metacognitively aware writers are able, in William Blake's' words, to "look thro it, & not with it" (qtd. in Berthoff 1978, 232). In other words, they engage in "thinking about thinking" (Berthoff 1978, 13). The need for metacognition assumes special importance when writers find themselves required to work in unfamiliar contexts or with forms with which they are unfamiliar. In those cases, metacognition allows writers to assess which skill and knowledge sets apply in these novel situations and which do not. In the end, while cognition remains critical to effective writing, it is metacognition that endows writers with a certain control over their work, regardless of the situation in which they operate.

Popular conceptions of what it means to write assume that knowledge of a subject (e.g., the history of the Civil War) is enough to produce a successful written report on that subject, or that knowledge of the rules of language, grammar, and mechanics is sufficient to produce an effective piece of written communication. In fact, cognition, while essential to thoughtful performance, cannot guarantee success, given the challenges of writing across disciplines, for varied audiences, and in diverse genres. It must be accompanied by metacognition.

5.3

HABITUATED PRACTICE CAN LEAD TO ENTRENCHMENT
Chris M. Anson

When writers' contexts are constrained and they are subjected to repeated practice of the same genres, using the same processes for the same rhetorical purposes and addressing the same audiences, their conceptual framework for writing may become entrenched, "solidified," or "sedimented." When this happens, they may try to apply that framework in a new or unfamiliar writing situation, resulting in a mismatch between what they produce and the expectations or norms of their new community (see 2.1, "Writing Represents the World, Events, Ideas, and Feelings," and 3.3, "Writing Is Informed by Prior Experience").

Repeated practice of the same mental task or activity can lead to what psychologists call *automaticity* or *unconscious competence*, the application of a process or the retrieval of information that doesn't require conscious attention (Van Nieuwerburgh and Passmore 2012). For example, among experienced drivers, the process of shifting gears becomes so habituated through repeated practice that it usually reaches a stage of automaticity, allowing drivers to do it while performing other tasks such as talking to a passenger and gauging the distance of the car from a stoplight. Although writing is far more complex than gear shifting, the principle of automaticity also applies. A veteran police officer who has written many hundreds of incident reports may apply habituated practices, such as being as highly objective as possible, in other situations that call for a different approach, such as sharing subjective impressions or using an elegant, elaborated style.

In writing, the misapplication of habituated practices often occurs among novice writers, such as those who are trained throughout high school to write five-paragraph-style essays for standardized tests (Anson 2008). Placed in a new situation where the audience, purpose, genre, and other aspects of writing may be very different from those required in five-paragraph themes, such writers may resort to their habituated practice and fail to meet the expectations of their new rhetorical community. Habituation also explains the struggles more proficient writers experience when they have practiced certain genres for years and then try to deploy their abilities in new settings. For example, even prolific academic writers who are highly skilled at producing research reports and articles may struggle to write in new or unfamiliar settings. A significant body of literature has accumulated around the problems associated with scientists who are unable to "translate" their complex knowledge and research findings for public audiences. Such translation requires consciously breaking with entrenched practices and being rhetorically flexible enough to think about how a text will be understood by a broader range of readers.

To counter the effects of habituation, some writing experts advocate a pedagogical approach that emphasizes rhetorical dexterity and an ability to confront new writing situations with a high degree of metacognition or rhetorical awareness learned through exposure to writing studies (Downs and Wardle 2012). Such awareness is said to help writers study and reflect on what they must to do in their writing to succeed by the standards of the community. There is some scholarly debate, however, about the effectiveness of this kind of pedagogy. Using theories of situated cognition, some writing experts argue that in spite of a high level of metacognitive awareness, writers will always have difficulty moving across disparate rhetorical communities and must always, to some degree, "learn anew" in unfamiliar settings (Russell 1995).

5.4

REFLECTION IS CRITICAL FOR WRITERS' DEVELOPMENT
Kara Taczak

Writers develop and improve with practice, time, and—among other things—reflecting throughout the process. Reflection is a mode of inquiry: a deliberate way of systematically recalling writing experiences to reframe the current writing situation. It allows writers to recognize what they are doing in that particular moment (cognition), as well as to consider why they made the rhetorical choices they did (metacognition) (see 5.1, "Writing Is an Expression of Embodied Cognition"). The combination of cognition and metacognition, accessed through reflection, helps writers begin assessing themselves as writers, recognizing and building on their prior knowledge about writing. This deliberate type of reflection centers on writers' ability to theorize and question areas such as their processes, practices, beliefs, attitudes, and understandings about writing, along with the ability to consider why they made the rhetorical choices they did (see Driscoll 2011; Sommers 2011; Yancey 1998). This ability to theorize and question is especially important for writers engaging in new or especially challenging tasks because it helps writers relocate the knowledge and practices acquired from one writing site to another (i.e., a writer might learn genre awareness in a first-year writing course and later relocate the awareness about genres in helping to create a business memo for an advertising course).

Reflection can be troublesome because for some writers, reflection isn't an integral part of their processes and practices. This may be because (1) writers believe reflection needs to happen after the fact rather than seeing it as a critical, rhetorical act within the process; (2) writers assume reflection happens naturally and without prompting; (3) writers think reflection *only* means considering how they *feel* about their writing; (4) some writers may never have been asked to reflect on their writing and thus may simply not think of doing so; and (5) some writers may not be developmentally ready to reflect. All of these suggest that reflection itself can be challenging; thus, such experiences with and misconceptions about reflection can result in writers who do not use reflection as an active and engaged part of their writing processes and who don't understand that reflection can benefit their development and success as writers.

Importantly, and as demonstrated by the other threshold concepts, many factors help ensure students' success with writing; however, almost any of these factors can depend upon writers' ability to use effective reflection as part of their writing processes. For example, writers who are more attuned to conscious reflection make "deeper choices" (2.0, "Writing Speaks to Situations through Recognizable Forms"); writers' identities are connected to various parts of their lives, including their histories, processes, and prior experiences, and using reflection allows them to tap into these as a way to become better writers (see 3.2, "Writers' Histories, Processes, and Identities Vary"; 3.3, "Writing Is Informed by Prior Experience"; and 3.4, "Disciplinary and Professional Identities Are Constructed Through Writing"); revision, which includes some amount of failure, becomes particularly helpful when writers reflect and learn from these experiences (see 4.1, "Text Is an Object Outside of Oneself that Can Be Improved and Developed").". 4.2, "Failure Can Be an Important Part of Writing Development"; 4.3, "Learning to Write Effectively Requires Different Kinds of Practice, Time, and Effort"; and 4.4, "Revision Is Central to Developing Writing"). Reflection has the unique ability to connect across the various threshold concepts because it offers writers the ability to be active agents of change, making meaningful contributions to any rhetorical exchange (see 5.1, "Writing Is an Expression of Embodied Cognition"; 5.2, "Metacognition Is Not Cognition").

Reflection allows writers to recall, reframe, and relocate knowledge and practices; therefore, it must be worked at in order to be most effectively learned and practiced.

References

Alcorn, Marshall. 2002. *Changing the Subject in English Class: Discourse and the Constructions of Desire.* Carbondale: Southern Illinois University Press.

Angeli, Elizabeth. 2015. "Three Types of Memory in Emergency Medical Services Communication." *Written Communication* 32 (1): 3–38.

Anson, Chris M. 2008. "Closed Systems and Standardized Writing Tests." *College Composition and Communication* 60 (1): 113–28.

Barber, Chris, Paul Smith, James Cross, John E. Hunter, and Richard McMaster. 2006. "Crime Scene Investigation as Distributed Cognition." In *Distributed Cognition*, ed. Stevan Harnad and Itiel E. Dror, special issue of *Pragmatics and Cognition* 14 (2): 357–85.

Bazerman, Charles. 2012. "Writing, Cognition, and Affect from the Perspectives of Sociocultural and Historic Studies of Writing." In *Past, Present, and Future Contributions of Cognitive Writing Research to Cognitive Psychology*, ed. Virginia W. Berninger, 89–104. New York: Psychology Press.

Bereiter, Carl, and Marlene Scardamalia. 1987. *The Psychology of Written Composition.* Hillsdale, NJ: Erlbaum.

Berninger, Virginia W., and T. Richards. 2012. "The Writing Brain: Coordinating Sensory/Motor, Language, and Cognitive Systems in Working Memory Architecture." In *Past, Present, and Future Contributions of Cognitive Writing Research to Cognitive Psychology*, edited by Virginia Berninger, 537–563. New York: Psychology Press.

Berninger, Virginia W., and William D. Winn. 2006. "Implications of Advancements in Brain Research and Technology for Writing Development, Writing Instruction, and Educational Evolution." In *Handbook of Writing Research*, edited by Charles A. MacArthur, Steve Graham, and Jill Fitzgerald, 96–114. New York: Guilford.

Berthoff, Ann E. 1978. *Forming, Thinking, Writing: The Composing Imagination.* Rochelle Park, NJ: Hayden.

Berthoff, Ann E. 1981. *The Making of Meaning: Metaphors, Models, and Maxims for Writing Teachers.* Upper Montclair, NJ: Boynton/Cook.

Bizzell, Patricia. 1982. "Cognition, Convention, and Certainty: What We Know and What We Need to Know About Writing." *Pre/Text* 3 (3): 213–43.

Bloom, Lynn Z. 1981. "Why Graduate Students Can't Write: Implications of Research on Writing Anxiety for Graduate Education." *JAC: Journal of Advanced Composition* 2.1 (2): 103–18.

Bridwell, Lillian S. 1980. "Revising Strategies in Twelfth Grade Students' Transactional Writing." *Research in the Teaching of English* 14:197–222.

Britton, James, Tony Burgess, Nancy Martin, Alex McLeod, and Harold Rosen. 1975. *The Development of Writing Abilities(11–18).* London: MacMillan.

Cooper, Marilyn M. 2011. "Rhetorical Agency as Emergent and Enacted." *College Composition and Communication* 62 (3): 420–49.

Downs, Douglas, and Elizabeth Wardle. 2012. "Teaching about Writing, Righting Misconceptions: (Re)Envisioning 'First-Year Composition' as 'Introduction to Writing Studies.'" *College Composition and Communication* 58 (4): 552–84.

Driscoll, Dana Lynn. 2011. "Connected, Disconnected, or Uncertain: Student Attitudes about Future Writing Contexts and Perceptions of Transfer from First Year Writing to the Disciplines." *Across the Disciplines* 8 (2). http://wac.colostate.edu/atd/articles/driscoll2011/index.cfm.

Elbow, Peter. 1981. *Writing with Power: Techniques for Mastering the Writing Process.* New York: Oxford University Press.

Flower, Linda, and John R. Hayes. 1981. "A Cognitive Process Theory of Writing." *College Composition and Communication* 32 (4): 365–87. http://dx.doi.org/10.2307/356600.

Gardner, Howard. 2008. *Frames of Mind: The Theory of Multiple Intelligences.* New York: Basic Books.

James, Karin H., and Laura Engelhardt. 2012. "The Effects of Handwriting Experience on Functional Brain Development in Pre-Literate Children." *Trends in Neuroscience and Education* 1 (1): 32–42. http://dx.doi.org/10.1016/j.tine.2012.08.001.

Kellogg, Ronald T. 2008. "Training Writing Skills: A Cognitive Developmental Perspective." *Journal of Writing Research* 1 (1): 1–26.

Lu, Min Zhan. 1999. "Importing 'Science': Neutralizing Basic Writing." In *Representing the "Other": Basic Writing and the Teaching of Basic Writing*, edited by Bruce Horner and Min Zhan Lu, 56–104. Urbana, IL: National Council of Teachers of English.

MacKay, Wendy E. 1999. "Is Paper Safe? The Role of Paper Flight Strips in Air Traffic Control." *ACM Transactions in Computer-Human Interaction (TOCHI)* 6 (4): 311–40.

Moffett, James. 1968. *Teaching the Universe of Discourse*. Upper Montclair, NJ: Boynton/ Cook.

Perl, Sondra. 1979. "The Composing Processes of Unskilled College Writers." *Research in the Teaching of English* 13 (4): 317–36.

Quinlan, Thomas, Maaike Loncke, Mariëlle Leijten, and Luuk Van Waes. 2012. "Coordinating the Cognitive Processes of Writing: The Role of the Monitor." *Written Communication* 29 (3): 345–68. http://dx.doi.org/10.1177/0741088312451112.

Richards, Todd L., Virginia W. Berninger, Pat Stock, Leah Altemeier, Pamala Trivedi, and Kenneth R. Maravilla. 2011. "Differences between Good and Poor Child Writers on fMRI Contrasts for Writing Newly Taught and Highly Practiced Letter Forms." *Reading and Writing* 24 (5): 493–516. http://dx.doi.org/10.1007/s11145-009-9217-3.

Rose, Mike, ed. 1985. *When a Writer Can't Write: Studies in Writer's Block and Other Composing-Process Problems*. New York: Guilford.

Russell, David. 1995. "Activity Theory and Its Implications for Writing Instruction." In *Reconceiving Writing, Rethinking Writing Instruction*, edited by Joseph Petraglia, 51–77. Mahwah, NJ: Erlbaum.

Soliday, Mary. 2002. *The Politics of Remediation: Institutional and Student Needs in Higher Education*. Pittsburgh: University of Pittsburgh Press.

Sommers, Jeff. 2011. "Reflection Revisited: The Class Collage." *Journal of Basic Writing* 30 (1): 99–129.

Sommers, Nancy. 1980. "Revision Strategies of Student Writers and Experienced Adult Writers." *College Composition and Communication* 31 (4): 378–88. http://dx.doi.org/10 .2307/356588.

Van Nieuwerburgh, Christian, and Jonathan Passmore. 2012. "Creating Coaching Cultures for Learning." In *Coaching in Education: Getting Better Results for Students, Educators, and Parents*, edited by Christian van Nieuwerburgh, 153–72. London: Karnac.

Vygotsky, Lev S. 1986. *Thought and Language*. Cambridge: MIT Press.

Yancey, Kathleen Blake. 1998. *Reflection in the Writing Classroom*. Logan: Utah State University Press.

INDEX